Decarbonising and Decolonising Economics

Ariane Agunsoye · Alexandra Arntsen
Editors

Decarbonising and Decolonising Economics

Why Climate Justice Demands Decolonising Decarbonisation

palgrave
macmillan

Editors
Ariane Agunsoye
Goldsmiths, University of London
London, UK

Alexandra Arntsen
Nottingham Trent University
Nottingham, UK

ISBN 978-3-032-11971-1 ISBN 978-3-032-11972-8 (eBook)
https://doi.org/10.1007/978-3-032-11972-8

This Palgrave Macmillan imprint is published by the registered company Springer Nature Switzerland AG
The registered company address is: Gewerbestrasse 11, 6330 Cham, Switzerland

Contents

List of Contributors

Ariane Agunsoye School of Creative Management, Goldsmiths, University of London, London, UK

Alexandra Arntsen Department of Economics, Nottingham Trent University, Nottingham, UK

Harshita Bhasin Institute for Human Development, New Delhi, India

Yannis Bougiatiotis Department of Economics, The New School for Social Research, New York, USA

Ying Chen Department of Economics, The New School for Social Research, New York, USA

Eurydice Fotopoulou Independent Researcher, London, UK

Yousef Ghorbani School of Natural Sciences, University of Lincoln, Lincoln, UK

Priya Lukka School of Politics and International Studies, University of Leeds, Leeds, UK

Glen T. Nwaila The African Research Centre for Ore Systems Science (CORES), School of Geosciences, University of the Witwatersrand, Johannesburg, South Africa

Helen Puntha School of Health and Medical Sciences, City St George's, University of London, London, UK

Derek Hugh Rose The African Research Centre for Ore Systems Science (CORES), University of the Witwatersrand, Johannesburg, South Africa

Melanie Gayana Welaratne Centre for Academic Development and Quality, Nottingham Trent University, Nottingham, UK

List of Figures

Decolonising Approaches to Decarbonisation Through Justice and Reparations

Navigating Mineral Intensity: Decolonising the Green Energy Transition

Introduction

Ariane Agunsoye and Alexandra Arntsen

Abstract This chapter introduces this book's central argument: climate justice necessitates the simultaneous processes of decarbonisation and decolonisation. It argues that the climate crisis has a crucial justice dimension, as its impacts, deeply rooted in colonial histories and capitalist exploitation, disproportionately affect the Global South. This calls for a critical re-examination of dominant economic models and climate policies through a decolonial lens, challenging Eurocentric paradigms and advocating for inclusive, pluralistic approaches to sustainability. The chapter outlines the structure of the book and introduces key themes such as justice, reparations, and ecological balance in the global transition to a low-carbon economy.

Keywords Decolonisation · Decarbonisation · Eurocentrism · Pluralistic economics

---

A. Agunsoye (✉)
School of Creative Management, Goldsmiths, University of London, London, UK
e-mail: A.Agunsoye@gold.ac.uk

A. Arntsen
Department of Economics, Nottingham Trent University, Nottingham, UK
e-mail: alexandra.arntsen@ntu.ac.uk

A. Agunsoye and A. Arntsen (eds.), *Decarbonising and Decolonising Economics*, https://doi.org/10.1007/978-3-032-11972-8_1

The notion of climate justice has gained prominence in recent years, emphasising that understanding the climate crisis requires addressing its historical roots in social injustices and considering non-Western theories of sustainable development. Colonisation has created a perverse paradox in which resources were extracted to fuel industrialisation, leading to over-exploitation and climate change, effects that disproportionately impact countries of the Global South. Present-day political, economic, scientific, and cultural theories are shaped by the colonial era, making it essential to investigate historical processes and their ongoing influence on mindsets, power relations, and climate. Re-examining economic systems and decarbonisation initiatives through a decolonial lens not only challenges the presumed neutrality and universality of dominant economic models, prompting a critical examination of their origins and consequences, but also reveals how colonialism and imperialism have enabled Western economic systems (which are inseparable from political structures), particularly capitalism, to be positioned as the only valid system. Replication of this system globally has led to a polarization of wealth, where a minority of people, often in the Global North, disproportionately benefit. Relatedly, the capitalist exploitation of natural resources, driven by the pursuit of profit, has directly contributed to climate change, as capitalism is systemically dependent on GDP growth, resource extraction and carbon-intensive production.

As a result of these dynamics, it is essential that decarbonisation and decolonisation need to be done simultaneously. Decolonising decarbonisation involves interrogating and dismantling the persistent colonial legacies, ideologies, and power dynamics that continue to shape global climate governance. The challenge of decolonisation advocates for a transformative shift towards climate policies and practices that are not only environmentally sustainable but also socially just, ensuring that the transition to a low-carbon economy equitably addresses the historical and contemporary marginalisation of the Global South. Within economics, this requires critical examination of how colonial power structures continue to influence contemporary climate policy and economic decision-making. Decolonising decarbonisation is therefore crucial to reducing negative impacts, losses and damages, particularly for communities and environments that have contributed least to climate change yet are disproportionately affected by it.

This book presents an overview of how the economics discipline and economic systems have approached these overlapping challenges of decolonisation and decarbonisation by asking the following questions: To what extent is the global decarbonisation agenda constrained by Western paradigms and theoretical frameworks? Can non-Western insights provide better ways of understanding and addressing climate change and why? How can the discipline of economics become more inclusive and better suited to the ecological demands of the twenty-first century? These questions are particularly relevant in the aftermath of recent challenges, which have intensified socio-economic inequalities and amplified calls for a just and sustainable recovery.

At the core of the book's argument is a call for a decolonial approach to decarbonisation that not only requires a diversity of viewpoints but also a critical confrontation with Eurocentrism within economics, visible in both its theoretical foundations and its practices. The book advocates for inclusive and pluralistic approaches that rethink how economic knowledge in the context of sustainability is defined, reproduced, and applied. Central to this project is the interrogation of how economics risks perpetuating injustice in its approach to sustainability if it ignores the systemic legacies of racism, sexism, and colonialism. The aim of this approach is to enable a decarbonisation approach that serves the majority of the globe, rather than privileging the interests of a limited few it (D-Econ, n.d.[1]).

The chapters address various dimensions of decarbonisation and decolonisation, moving from the economics discipline itself to the power dynamics inherent in the economic system and to current practical approaches for tackling climate change. In line with a decolonial approach, we asked authors to provide a positionality statement, recognising that identities, upbringings, and educational backgrounds inevitably shape how we understand and interpret the world. Recognising this, we offer joint, yet individually nuanced, positionality statements to acknowledge our perspectives, biases, and potential blind spots. The decision of whether and how to provide such a statement was left with the authors. They are provided verbatim below.

Following the introduction chapter, Priya Lukka argues that addressing the climate crisis requires acknowledging the historical and ongoing inequalities rooted in colonisation and neoliberalism. Her chapter advocates for a decolonial approach to decarbonisation that incorporates interdisciplinary perspectives, historical repair, and broader notions of

[1] Available at: https://d-econ.org/mission/.

climate justice. 'Looking at the injustices of the world and its impacts, I am aware that I have a role in changing that through my actions. I recognise that my freedom and safety are simply because of when and where I was born. I stand in solidarity with and seek to elevate the ideas and visions of movements who imagine the world differently.'

Ying Chen and Yannis Bougiatiotis then examine the interconnected crises of climate change, the inadequacy of mainstream economics, and the developmental challenges of the Global South, critiquing dominant and alternative economic discourses for their methodological limitations and North-centric biases. The chapter argues that frameworks such as ecological colonialism and ecological imperialism offer deeper insights into these crises, providing a foundational step towards decarbonising and decolonising the discipline of economics. Chen's 'work explores the contradictions within capitalism and how they exhibit themselves. Topics she has studied include economic development, labor, and climate change, with a special focus on the Global South. Bougiatiotis' research focuses on International Economics, Regional Integration, Renewables and Green Industrial Policy with particular emphasis on the dynamics and economic, social and environmental implications of uneven development. Their work has been recognised in international journals as well as in intergovernmental organisations.'

Chapter 4 moves onto the structure of the global food system, exploring competing visions for a sustainable and resilient food system in response to agriculture's ecological impact and climate vulnerability. Harshita Basin critiques the mainstream, tech-driven approach for ignoring capitalism's role in ecological degradation and highlights food sovereignty and agroecology as transformative alternatives that centre justice, local autonomy, and ecological balance while acknowledging the political and economic barriers to their implementation. 'As an urban-based scholar from a privileged caste in India who studies rural and agrarian contexts, I critically reflect on the biases, blind spots and power relations that emanate from my position. My perspective on decarbonisation is informed by postcolonial critiques of the Eurocentric climate discourse as well as the layered inequalities which characterise postcolonial societies.'

Chapter 5 explores the growing reliance on critical minerals in the renewable energy transition, highlighting how current extractive practices often reproduce colonial patterns and deepen global inequalities. Yousef Ghorbani, Glen T. Nwaila, and Derek Hugh Rose advocate for decolonised, community-led approaches to mineral governance, emphasising equity, sustainability, and Indigenous knowledge, to achieve a just and regenerative energy future. 'As professionals spanning academia and industry, we bring expertise in energy materials, economic geology, geometallurgy, and process mineralogy. Our collective work, from mineral systems science and spatial data intelligence to supply chain integration and resource processing, advances a holistic understanding of critical materials. Grounded in both global and local contexts, we are committed to supporting mineral security and enabling a just and practical energy transition.'

Chapter 6 moves onto infrastructure systems, critiquing the absence of a universally accepted definition of infrastructure, highlighting how dominant (Western) interpretations, focused on physical sectors like transport, energy, and mining, shape global measurement standards and contribute to biased understandings of development. It argues that this narrow definition overlooks social infrastructure (e.g., healthcare, education, and care services), which is crucial for inclusive growth, gender equality, and sustainable development. By proposing an expanded, feminist-informed definition, the chapter underscores the dual benefits of social infrastructure: its lower carbon footprint and its potential to support decolonial and equitable development agendas. 'Eurydice Fotopoulou is an economist and an independent researcher working with the use of non-traditional data and AI. Previously, she was the head of non-financial assets development at the UK Office for National Statistics. Eurydice has worked in academia and as a consultant in the private sector and charities. She holds a Ph.D. in Economics from the University of Greenwich.'

The final chapter discusses approaches to decolonisation and decarbonisation in the context of the economics curriculum. It argues that the interconnected challenges of decolonisation and the dismantling of carbon-intensive, environmentally degrading systems should be addressed together. The chapter was written collaboratively by three practitioners from different backgrounds: 'I identify as a Brown, Sri Lankan/British, cis-woman. Growing up across seven countries has shaped my global perspective and deepened my understanding of identity, privilege, and belonging' (Melanie Gayana Welaratne). 'I am a white, English woman living and working in the UK; a high income, high carbon-emitting nation' (Helen Puntha). 'I identify as a White, Swedish cis-woman, living and working in the UK' (Alexandra Arntsen). We critically reflect on our positionality and the ongoing impact of coloniality on our life and communities, while striving to use our privileges to advocate for justice and equity.

Decolonising Approaches to Decarbonisation Through Justice and Reparations

Priya Lukka

Abstract In strategies towards a decarbonised world, the need to examine inequalities that have been produced by histories of colonisation and ongoing neoliberalism is important. This chapter explores the relationality between histories and practices towards imagining the world differently for climate outcomes, building on arguments for an interdisciplinary perspective of climate justice. The discussion considers what a decolonial shift could offer in the pursuit of climate justice, which includes a focus on decarbonisation and beyond. It argues that historical acknowledgement and considerations of repair should become of greater relevance for a framework of ideas for decolonial decarbonisation moving ahead.

Keywords Climate justice · Decarbonisation · Decolonisation · Reparations · Just transition

P. Lukka (✉)
School of Politics and International Studies, University of Leeds, Leeds, UK
e-mail: ptplu@leeds.ac.uk

A. Agunsoye and A. Arntsen (eds.), *Decarbonising and Decolonising Economics*, https://doi.org/10.1007/978-3-032-11972-8_2

1 Introduction

The ecological crisis is not reducible to emissions and pollution. Biodiversity loss, dispossession, displacement, extinction, ecocide, and ecosystem crisis are as critical (UN News, 2024). Their overall impact is exacerbating patterns of disadvantage for people, communities and countries. The differential impacts of climate change were noted by the Intergovernmental Panel on Climate Change (IPCC) in its 6th Assessment Report (of Working Group I), which sets out that the world will exceed the Paris Goal to limit global warming to 1.5 °C over pre-industrial levels by 2035 due to the widespread, rapid and growing nature of climate change:

> Regions and peoples with development constraints have high vulnerability to climatic hazards…with the largest adverse impacts in Asia, Africa, Central and South America, LDCs, Small Islands and the Arctic. (IPCC, 2023, p. 5).

Alongside this overall assessment, in 2022, the IPCC cited historical and ongoing patterns of inequity and colonialism as a driver of vulnerability to climate change for both ecosystems and people. This recognition is significant. It is a long overdue acknowledgement of a world that remains steeped in extractive mechanisms. Coloniality has also impacted and limited the solutions available to tackle climate change. Mohamed Adow, founder of Power Shift Africa, in discussing contemporary proposals for climate mitigation recognises the models of indebtedness that go with them:

> Sixty years ago, African countries attained their independence. We were able to kick colonisers out of our land. What they're doing now is basically introducing this new form of colonialism. (Lankaweb, 2023)

In light of contemporary approaches to tackling climate change, this discussion explores the relationality between histories and practices towards imagining the world differently, building on arguments for climate justice (Upham et al., 2022). Given the glaring realities of climate conditions and their resulting devastation, the urgent need to redefine our industrial and agricultural practices is framed as the process of decarbonisation. A fair process to achieve a decarbonised future has been termed the Just Transition by movements and activists pushing for equitable approaches to decarbonisation. This term initially emerged from the global trade union movement on the premise that the share of benefits from the economy were matters of interests for workers as citizens who are concerned with social justice (Stevis & Felli, 2015). These debates naturally combined the issue of labour rights with environmental justice. Just Transition coalitions advocate for disrupting monopoly ownership and control of energy production and re-imagine the future of workers and communities that have been reliant on the fossil fuel industry (Shelton & Eakin, 2022). This offers an understanding of people and communities harmed by the corporate control of their habitual environments. A grave example of such harm was seen in an environmental catastrophe in 2017 in London. Grenfell Tower, a high-rise social housing estate in London, UK, burned down due to a lack of environmental safety standards, leading to 72 deaths. The building lacked smoke alarms, sprinkler systems, and suitable escape routes (Danewid, 2020). Residents had complained about the building's dangerous living conditions and neglect of health and safety legislation (Grenfell Action Group, 2016) for many years but had been ignored by the local council. A refurbishment project carried out in 2017 covered the building in cheap and combustible cladding materials (Griffin, 2017). In July 2022, the United Nations General Assembly declared access to a clean, healthy, and sustainable environment a universal human right, recognising that environmental damage negatively impacts all human rights for present and future generations (UN Resolution A/76/L.75, 2022). Such rights for Grenfell dwellers came too late, and of those who survived, there are many long-term impacts. The stewardship of the environment is beyond science-based targets and includes safeguards for environmental standards and ensuring broader community well-being and safety.

A decolonial approach offers a way of examining inequalities that have been produced by histories of colonisation and ongoing neoliberalism. The hierarchy of people determined by markers such as race, gender, class, and sexuality, amongst others, becomes relevant as do the geographies and locations of people marginalised and minoritised by historical oppression. Conceptualised by Frantz Fanon (1961), to break free from structures of colonial control, decolonisation enables us to understand the legacies of hierarchical and racialised policies. This has been further elaborated by scholars such as Mignolo (2007), who argues that there is a constant reproduction of coloniality in the structures of today's world. Decoloniality provides a basis for understanding the historical origins and ongoing dynamics in which approaches to economic development are decided. Its theorists remind us that White supremacy, heteropatriarchy, racism, xenophobia, nationalism, militarism, and authoritarianism are all facets of a wider system of economic control (de Sousa Santos, 2021). A decolonial approach is important in the challenging journey towards decarbonisation. This discussion considers what a decolonial shift could offer in the pursuit of climate justice, with a focus on decarbonisation and beyond.

2 Decarbonising with Respect to Decoloniality

The transition to a low-carbon economy and its developmental pathway are the main facets of a decarbonisation strategy. The process of achieving sustainability, described as a net-zero emissions world, is through the pursuit of low-carbon development and a low-carbon transition (Wimbadi & Djalante, 2020). However, decarbonisation strategies should also be widened to reflect on the reasons for our current inability to live within planetary boundaries. This would be based on a historical analysis to inform de- and low-carbon transitions, based on a fuller understanding of the surpassing of planetary boundaries. Six of the nine Anthropocene processes that are critical for maintaining the stability and resilience of the Earth, such as freshwater use and atmospheric aerosol loading, are currently untenable. This means that we are beyond a scientifically based operating space for humanity that can safeguard an interglacial state and its resilience (Stockholm Resilience Centre, n.d.; Richardson et al., 2023). However, these planetary boundaries have not been surpassed only because of recent or post-colonial development and extraction. Both historical colonial expansion and ongoing exploitation are relevant. Decarbonisation should be rooted in a historical re-appraisal of the evidence of the culpability of cumulative emissions, as tracked from 1850 (Fig. 1, Carbon Brief, 2021), showing a dominant extraction pathway by the US.

This kind of analysis is a tool of decolonisation for rethinking wealth and asset redistribution and political power by illustrating the impact of colonialism and Transatlantic Slavery. Using this approach, the data on fossil extractivism demonstrates that there is a link between the past and present, as noted:

> ...the continued exploitation of the former colonies and peoples of the Third World...is both a continuation of the old imperialism as well as

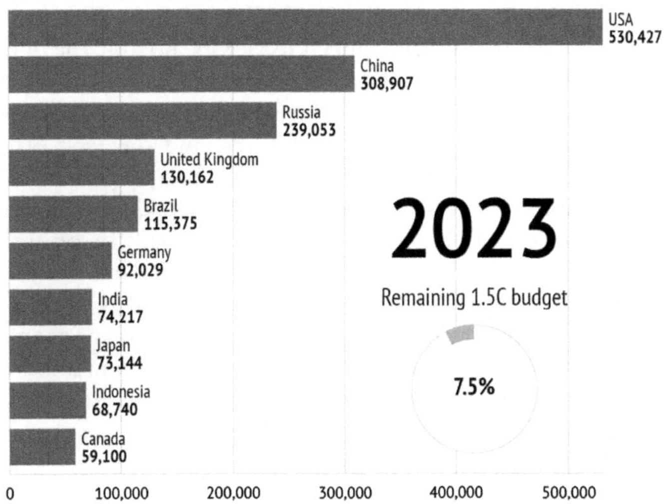

Fig. 1 Historical responsibility for climate change: cumulative CO_2 emissions from fossil fuels, land use and forestry, 1850–2023, million tonnes. *Source* Carbon Brief analysis

> forming an essential part of the fossil fuel economy that threatens our planet. (Cushion, 2021, p. 28).

Thus, decarbonisation needs to include an introspection of the unfair basis to historical industrialisation, as explained in the case of the British Empire and its use of violence and military power to dominate colonised countries:

> They (Britain[1]) approached the ruler of a non-European country and asked for access to its customers and its raw materials. If the country in question agreed, the British established themselves and started buying and selling. But if the country refused, the British would threaten military action. In some cases, the natives eventually gave in and signed a commercial treaty, often referred to as an unequal treaty. In other cases, when the natives stood their ground, the result was war. (Ringmar, 2019, p. 178)

[1] *Author's clarification.*

In a wider historical re-appraisal, the origins of European and North American capitalism are explicitly linked to factors, notably the oppression of African people, who were transported to the Americas. The experiences of people in Europe and the UK, who were forced off their land and driven into new industrial cities by enclosures, and the First Nations of North America and Australia who saw their land expropriated and were the victims of genocide are also relevant (Cushion, 2021). A strategic link between the impacts of climate change and the need for repair for the impacts of Transatlantic slavery and colonialism is understood through a recognition of the impact of land and asset theft and of forced migration and labour on afflicted groups. This acknowledgement should be of greater relevance for a framework on decolonial decarbonisation moving ahead. Such a framework would be driven by how we understand the diverging inequalities between countries. The comparative experience of countries under colonialism demarks the delineations, corresponding to social, environmental, and economic disparities, of the world today. This means that there is core and periphery of countries,[2] broadly correlating to colonisers or colonised geographies. This demarcation does not assume that one grouping is better in development or living standards than the other. However, it does recognise that core countries drive the structures and governance that dominate countries that are peripheralised. Or, in other words, that the exploitative socio-political structures (Gattey, 2021) of core countries oppress peripheralised countries.

This construction of global divisions is often used interchangeably with notions of "a developed North and the under-developed South" (Narayanaswamy et al., 2021, p. 3). When we try to unpack why colonial pathways of extractivism have been possible, an awareness of the knowledge hierarchies is needed. In a decolonial framework, we recognise that knowledge, and ways of working from countries considered part of the "North" have often been viewed or presented as intrinsically more valuable than those of local and indigenous communities and/or knowledge from what is termed the Southern hemisphere (Osofisan, 2020). The reason for this unescapable infusion of knowledge from the Northern to Southern hemisphere relates to categorisations and assessments by the former of the latter. The narrative of a so-called development gap between "rich and poor" countries was used to accelerate a doctrine of economic

[2] This is the way in which countries will be described in the rest of this discussion, except where otherwise described in works.

modernisation. This involved "underdeveloped" countries transforming their economies towards models and processes of industrialisation as had occurred in core or developed countries. This process of industrialisation has tried to dismantle existing local economic structures and traditional cultures. Within this, a model of ecological colonialism has pushed fossil fuel industries and extraction- and deforestation-based economies onto former colonised countries (Adelman, 2020). In the context of the Amazon rainforest and its ongoing land-use conversion and exposure to climate change, reviews of data have found that anthropogenic changes are occurring much faster than naturally occurring environmental changes of the past. The deforestation and land-use change in the Amazon and elsewhere has made a significant contribution to the cumulative total of CO^2 (as shown in the level of historical emissions for Brazil in Fig. 1). The overall carbon budget has been used up at an accelerating pace, with half the cumulative total since 1850 having been released over the past 40 years (Carbon Brief, 2021, Lapola, 2023).

In fact, industrialisation was part of a much wider system of ongoing control from core countries who drove colonial expansion. This was the economic strategy of neocolonialism in which the colonial system continued to thrive, in the form of indirect and coercive forms of domination by political, economic, social, and military means, despite formal independence (Martin, 1985). The twentieth century saw a dismantling of colonialism's operations, but its logic and organisation of governance and unequal power relations continue to prevail. It is closely linked to the post-colonial practice of using globalisation, and the promise of financial aid to gain political influence in less developed countries (Longley, 2021). Although colonised countries had gained political "independence", many of the economic power structures, processes, and mechanisms that enabled colonial exploitation left an enduring effect of discrimination, inequality, and poverty (Acemoglu et al., 2000; Prashad, 2007). Throughout neocolonialism, from the 1950s onwards, there were imposed policies over newly independent countries through the development of global trading networks that had a profound impact on the world (Ringmar, 2019). For example, in trading with East Asia, each trading company was given a monopoly on trade with a particular part of the world to enable lucrative profits to be earnt. For the monarchical rulers of Europe, they could borrow money from the trading companies for their own investments. Ringmar (2019) argues that this is how the Bank of England in the UK and similar financial institutions came to be established, many of which became the centre of international finance system.

In the 1970s, an investment boom in peripheralised countries eventually led to a debt bubble for many of these countries. This was because the loans from core countries had interest rates that increased over time and made it challenging for peripheralised countries to repay, which was the start of a structural debt crisis for these countries (Muchhala, 2022). Understanding current climate vulnerabilities as a legacy is understood by considering the accompanying policy decisions made for countries. From the 1980s onwards, there have been ongoing mechanisms of coloniality in the form of structural adjustment policies, specifying extractive trade, export, and financing measures that have been imposed on low-income countries (Patnaik et al., 2021). This included the liberalisation of trade, eradicating fixed prices for essential items and ending state subsidies. The global expansion of markets promised greater prosperity with globalisation, vis a vis trade and financial integration. This is where the policies of the IMF and the World Bank began to further shape coloniality. In the 1990s, structural adjustment programmes from the IMF and the World Bank led to the provision of loans for coping with debt challenges that began in the 1970s, in exchange for the implementation of certain policy measures, bringing the advent of a neoliberal agenda (Zajontz, 2022). These policies also reduced the power of labour as vast profits began to be created from cross-border trading (Smith, 2016), as the opening of national stock markets was a conditionality to receive such loans.

Each phase has compounded the power dynamics of earlier more overt colonialism. The neoliberal agenda has meant free markets, foreign investments, and privatisation. The global economy has since been organised to facilitate powerful countries' access to cheap labour and raw materials (Hickel, 2020). Ongoing asymmetries related to dollar hegemony are noted (Dymski, 2021), as loans were mostly issued in the US dollar and thus made recipient countries cyclically vulnerable to the US economy's upturns and downturns. Even now, vulnerable countries face a structural dependency on international financing which exacerbates and squeezes their ongoing need for climate finance (Muchhala, 2022). In tracking policy over time, decarbonising becomes about understanding a purposeful policy choice towards industrialised development designed by core countries for periphery countries. The aggressive pathway to industrialisation was not something that periphery countries had chosen for themselves. Yet, the contentious issue of culpability for resulting environmental degradation remains unresolved (Gattey, 2021). Who should forego remaining fossil fuel usage is unreconciled, despite data indicating a destructive emitter record by America and the EU 27 countries (Fig. 2).

An acknowledgement of the harm that has been caused by capitalist expansion is acutely needed as many countries contend with precarious climatic conditions (United Nations, 2024) and many other injustices that are the symptoms and consequences of capitalist development. In response to planetary challenges resulting from fossil fuel colonialism, the Asian Peoples Movement for Debt and Development (APMDD) calls for the cancellation of climate debt and has coined the notion of "'ecological debt' as they explain below:

> There is a larger picture and a longer history of debt domination going back to the waves of colonisation that saw the North accumulating power and wealth by dispossessing all of us through oppression and plunder. This is a huge, unpayable debt of the North to the South caused by centuries of extractivism that damaged not only the ecosystems within our national borders but the planet as a whole. We call this the ecological debt, which is the accumulated debt by Northern industrialized countries owed to the South from resource plundering, environmental destruction and the unhampered occupation of the environment to dump wastes, including the dumping of carbon into the atmosphere. It also represents a debt to future generations who now face greater threats to their survival in the face

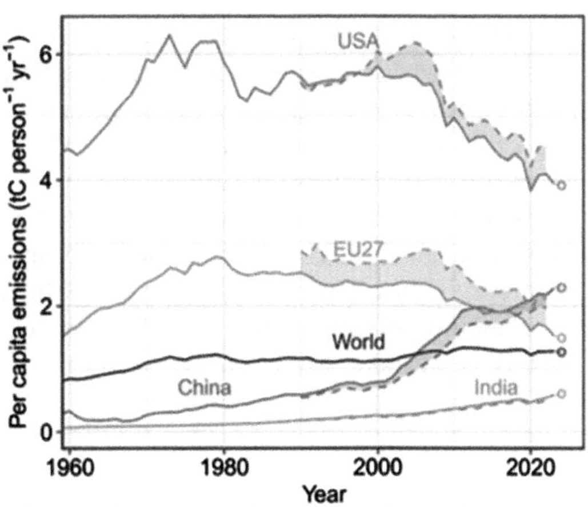

Fig. 2 Fossil CO_2 emissions across the world, historically. *Source* Global Carbon Budget 2024, amalgamated analysis produced by Friedlingstein et al., (2024)

> of the planetary emergency brought by climate change. (APMDD, 2025, p. 5).

This illustrates a justice-driven and radical demand for change. The APMDD articulates its calls for justice through demanding systems change, including of the global financial architecture that governs economies and the rules around environmental extraction (APMDD, 2025). Related calls to justice also demand an end to ongoing exposure to militarism, food crises, recurring debt-financial crises (Lapavitsas & Soydan, 2022), and unequal exchange in the trading of goods and services. The impact of this is that people everywhere are suffering from increasingly acute socioeconomic challenges with escalating inflation and an erosion of living standards (UN DESA, 2022). For former colonised countries, reclaiming sovereignty seems unreachable, unless a fundamental shift to repair, as will be discussed, is embedded in climate and debt justice approaches.

3 The Limitations of a Degrowth Approach

Decarbonisation debates have evolved to offer alternative ideas on economic growth and its centrality as a measure of societal progress. The rationale of the neoliberal model was the improvement it would bring in living standards. While the annual rate of global GDP growth has averaged around 3 per cent over the past decade (World Bank, 2022), income inequality has exacerbated (Chancel et al., 2022). This widening gap has resulted in social exclusion. There are deprived groups across the world who are significantly worse off than counterparts on several factors such as race, gender, ethnicity, and class. Otele (2009) discusses disparities between indentured people who were made slaves from the Asian sub-continent, plantation owners, and people from Africa who were made slaves that have persisted post-colonialism. In the US, financial estimates at a household level show significant wealth gaps, notably a difference of median hourly earnings of $5.12 between Black and White workers and an average loss of $1930 per Black labour force participant[3] (Darity & Mullen, 2022). More specifically, Donaghy et al. (2023) detail

[3] For 2019.

how public health hazards from air and water pollution and risks associated with climate change in the US fall disproportionately on racial and other marginalised groups.

Coming back to the idea that GDP lifts all boats equally, the reality is that growth does not translate into increased wellbeing uniformly or for most households across the world. Instead, the gains of growth have been concentrated in extreme wealth creation (World Bank, 2021) rather than the provision of an adequate standard of living for people experiencing poverty and a lack of equality and opportunity. Indeed, the global poverty reduction since the Cold War has been mostly about moving people from below to not far above a low poverty threshold (Sumner et al., 2021), based on a neoclassical theory of poverty eradication that emphasises monetary aspects. This contrasts with Marxian theories on poverty which consider class and discrimination as central to tackling a person's deprivation alongside their poverty status (Davis & Sanchez-Martinez, 2015). Income inequality has risen since the introduction of neoliberal policies, driven by widening gaps in labour income and more recently in the income generated from assets (Konczal et al., 2022). It is argued that this has allowed an elite richest 1% of the global population, to become responsible for decisions about 59% of the world's global financial assets, including resource extraction, globalised production, investment, and energy production and use (Oxfam, 2024; Perkins, 2019). Worryingly, decision-making about environmental matters has become a captured space.

In addition to the skewed gains from growth, there is a substantial body of new economy thinking, reflective of sustainability constraints posed by rapid rates of environmental degradation and humanitarian crises resulting from climate change. In this context, decarbonisation has a specific focus on not just a time urgency but the need for a focus on consumption models and citizenship relating to what individual action should be. A degrowth approach examines consumption levels and proposes their reduction, towards the broader strategy of staying within planetary boundaries. Concepts for de-growth through tackling the "...conflict between growth and ecology" (Hickel, 2020, p. 163) and "circularity" (Raeworth, 2011, p. 37), have become planks of economic development discussions. At the centre of ideas for degrowth is a commitment to support pathways towards more equitable and sustainable futures by decreasing quantities of resources and energy used by wealthy economies (Paulson, 2024).

The argument for curbing consumption has been posed as a possible strategy for periphery countries too. However, it is incompatible to conceive of consumption reduction for countries where basic human rights for essential survival are not yet fulfilled, such as the right to affordable food and healthcare. From a decolonial perspective, there are limitations with the concept of degrowth. It is argued that harnessing technological transformation is one way through which degrowth could be progressed. This would involve the large-scale expansion of Western technology and moving away from traditional forms of industrial production. However, it is questionable if countries that are peripheralised are ready for such a scaling back of labour towards technology-based economies (Paulson, 2024). That is unless education and training opportunities are created to support such a transition, and sufficient alternative jobs are available for people who may be unemployed as a result. Paulson (2024, p. 83) highlights that high-income countries are being urged to provide remedy to the situation of historical harms due to their own culpability:

> ...high-income societies would do better to focus on decreasing their own consumption and accumulation; repaying ecological debts; and reversing unequal flows of capital, resources, and waste.

Countries adhering to a post-growth model might face challenges in competing with nations that prioritise economic expansion, potentially impacting their geopolitical influence and economic competitiveness. The idea that the agenda for moderating an approach to growth can be set by countries that once extracted from the same set of formerly colonised countries raises further concerns from a decolonial perspective. There should be principles of solidarity in considering who has caused damage and who should repair for this harm in the context of remaining fossil fuel-led expansion. Any attempt to tackle the climate crisis must consider the inequality that has been generated both by neo-colonialism and by the nature of how the climate crisis is affecting the world's most vulnerable regions. Here, frameworks for working out a shared responsibility have used the concept of common but differentiated responsibility. However, while such approaches might recognise that previous European colonisers, such as Germany and the UK, account for 4% and 3% of the global total of CO^2 emissions (Carbon Brief, 2021), such calculations do not include the emissions caused in periphery countries by core countries. Neither do they assign responsibility for them. Climate justice as a praxis of solidarity and collective action (Sultana, 2022) is important, therefore, for moving us beyond binaries of North and South and taking conceptualities of repair into global debates.

4 Distributional Impacts and Repair

"Present wrongs require acknowledgment of and restitution for past injustices" (Lahiri & Darity, 2024, p. 676). Widening the perspective of decarbonisation, brings us to the concept of a Just Transition. This is rooted in a sense of justice where the equitable distribution of the benefits and costs of the transition away from high carbon and unsustainable development are considered (Upham et al., 2022). In this perspective, three forms of justice are relevant (Upham et al., 2022). Firstly, distributional justice considers the benefits and burdens across different groups using the approaches of rights, duties and equitable approaches to resource mobilisation for climate justice. Secondly, procedural justice, as seeking a fair, equitable, and inclusive process of all who choose to participate, is relevant. Thirdly, the historical relationality of justice, as understanding and acknowledging historic and ongoing inequalities and thus obligations across temporalities is of importance. This includes repair-based approaches for harm caused in the past and trying to stop the harm of the present use of fossil fuels, as illustrated in the campaign for reparations for ecological debt, as earlier discussed (APMDD, 2025).

These three approaches give a wider strategic framework for re-envisioning decarbonisation through decoloniality. It also broadens the perspective to consider distributional ideas for justice. Kim (2023) argues a need to justify the distribution of reparative obligations for historical injustice amongst present-day agents. Benefits that demand redress are the occupation by countries or elite groups of powerful and privileged positions within contemporary social structures, especially where structures are the legacy of major historical injustices namely Transatlantic Slavery and colonialism. This leads to the case for beneficiaries to support and enact various reforms to the social structures that produce unjust outcomes for historically marginalised groups today.

Recognising culpability for colonial damage in the past and the present is reflected in the growing space for notions of repair in climate change debates. The uneven effects of colonial damage have become an important way of appraising the situation facing many countries with low-level technical adaptation for dealing with climate outcomes (Grasso, 2024). Climate change is seen as an issue of equity as much as it is one of technical capability. However, the vulnerability and lack of preparation facing particular countries is not coincidental. Colonial histories and accompanying racialised economic policies leave minoritised groups as the victims of anthropogenic climate change and the least empowered in their preparedness (Mercer & Simpson, 2023). Debates on reparations, as offered by Perry (2021) and Táíwò (2022), have challenged a view that climate change affects everyone in the same way and suggest a range of policies towards repair. Táíwò (2022) argues for a global climate fund involving debt relief, recognising that wealthy sections of society have inherited more from the racial empire of fossil fuel. Such an argument takes us into wider interpretations of reparations that strive to re-balance in light of colonially delineated power structures.

This brings us to a specific appreciation of climate justice as achieved through climate reparations. Obeng-Odoom (2023) argues that without ecological reparations, no levels of alternative development, limits to growth/degrowth, fair exchange, or Just Transition will be sufficient. Táíwò (2022) sets out an approach that considers specific aims for climate reparations. This includes providing unconditional cash transfers at a national level. Global justice demands like progressive taxation for redistribution and eradicating tax havens to end the hiding of money that could be available for climate finance become relevant here. Distributional and repair-based approaches recognise harm is experienced in different ways for countries that were once colonised, with a focus on the rights of affected communities impacted and vulnerabilised by environmental crises and degradation. This takes us forward from policies that are designed with neutrality for the harms experienced across different groups living in destitution (Kothari, 2006). Such ahistorical approaches, common in the international development sector, ignore the racialised impacts of industrialisation. This is relevant because *who* is particularly vulnerable to the negative impacts of climate change is vital to better understand. The language of development is significant here. "Race" has seemingly been rejected, and has been replaced by ideas such as developed, underdeveloped and developing. In part, this has led to the invisibility of racial injustice.

We need more ideas for equity-distributing life for people across the planet that address the inequalities that groups affected by and living the detrimental legacy of Transatlantic Slavery and colonialism face. There is a racial unevenness of the capitalist system that has largely been ignored in economic discourse. Capital, land, and property were accumulated through the power of vested interests and denied along lines of racial subjugation. Brissett (2025) argues that extractive capitalism, as choreographed by Western countries solidified racial capitalism. Ideas about primitive accumulation of capital have been pioneered by many scholars. Patnaik (2015) argues, with reference to Marxian perspectives on workers and capital (1921), that in neoliberal capitalism even without formal colonial structures there is a basic tendency of capitalism towards an increasing inequality of income distribution between workers and large capitalists. These polarising tendencies are manifest in racially delineated ways such as the market structures that enable real wages in former colonised countries to remain at near-subsistence levels (Patnaik, 2015). This is further addressed in the work of Akala (The Guardian, 2018), who draws out that under capitalism, racialised people have been relegated into lower realms of humanity. This brings us to the idea that racism has been a much more fundamental strategy of evolving post-War and ongoing capitalist modernity. Koram (2022) argues in fact that effective anti-racism requires a confrontation with the ruling trends of capitalism and sees reparations as a way of the agendas of anti-capitalism and anti-racism intertwining, as widely discussed in other literature too (Koshy et al., 2022; Kundnani, 2023).

5 From Decarbonisation to Justice

From a decolonial perspective, the justice of the present is a function of the justice of the past (Macklem, 2005). Its pursuit is multi-faceted. Justice is achieved, as history would demonstrate, through people and their movements fighting for change and resisting structures that serve the interests of powerful and elite groups. Remedy for harm is brought about through: "a way of acknowledging historic wrongs and accounting for them" (Bhambra, 2022, p. 231). This discussion extends a challenge for decarbonisation to reconcile ongoing coloniality. This can be achieved through reparative justice. Throughout history, reparations have been pursued by people, groups, and communities that have often been agents of change in interrogating structural power relations, and factors that perpetuate the exclusion of marginalised, minoritised and excluded people. A repair-based approach acknowledges the experience of harm and the impact of policies to extract surplus from former colonial states resulting in unjust enrichment at the cost of oppressed communities. Repair includes the restoration of people's dignity and working in solidarity with communities who have experienced harm.

Reflecting on the dichotomies of how economics is practised and the urgency and need for more responsive policies that save lives, Táíwò (2022, p. 158) suggests that climate policies become more reflective and responsive to the colonial exploitations that have created an economic model that deprioritised environmental sustainability:

> ...our response to climate crisis will deeply determine the possibilities for justice (and injustice) in what remains of this century – and if we survive to the next: Had some things gone differently even decades ago – had the countries and corporations of the Global North polluted less, had the fossil fuel interests not worked along with coal and freight rail companies to orchestrate misinformation campaigns, protecting their short-term financial gains at the cost of their and our collective future – the relationship between reparations and climate crisis could well have been quite different.

In Táíwò's perspective, if we recognise that colonialism has led to deep and continuing inequalities, there is a rationale to redistribute both wealth and power which then creates the conditions for climate justice. Redistribution rather than aid or concessional finance could create a more substantial response to our current challenges of an unsustainable existence and surpassing planetary boundaries. Climate justice also considers issues of healing. Scholar activist Karenga (2022) says that reparations is about remaking, renewing and repairing the world. In a speech for Indigenous Liberation Day 2022 by movement leader, Esther Xosei, she said that reparations are holistic:

> Repair is not money, which is what the talk about reparations has become. It's been reduced to a finite. It doesn't matter how much trillions...it doesn't matter how much that is. That is only 1% of what reparations is about. ...Reparations are necessary because colonization continues. Colonialism continues. Land dispossession continues. Genocide continues. Ecocide continues. This is why reparations are necessary. Reparations is about taking back our world.

Reparations have the capacity to probe at a current world order marred by inequalities. The objective of a reparations project is "to redress the socioeconomic inequalities associated with race" (Darity & Mullen, 2020, p. 240). Some forms of reparations are rooted in the idea of planet repairs as coined by activists and scholars in the pan-Afrikan reparations movement where there is an interconnection between cognitive justice, reparatory justice, and environmental justice (Chinweizu, 1993). In this approach, there is a focus on how we are in relationship to one another, to the planet, to our ancestors, and to spiritual knowledge. Restoration (returning to original position), restitution (restoring lost items like land), and rehabilitation (restoring from damage) fall under this framing. While some of the debates on reparations focus on the need to acknowledge harm caused by institutions and states and the sums that should be paid, there are broader concepts of reparations that are richly intertwined with anti-colonial perspectives, that demand radical and justice-driven change (Stanford-Xosei, 2019).

The broad notion of reparations refers to disclosure and acknowledgement of the truth about violations, responsibilities, the accountability of perpetrators through justice, and guarantees of non-repetition. A loss of cultural identity is relevant. For example, the theft of Indigenous lands in Australia and North America, amongst other places, and the violence committed against Indigenous peoples to build capitalism across countries is well-recognised (Pieratos & Two Bulls, 2021). Activism around Land Back is about reclaiming Indigenous spheres of influence and sovereignty. These notions apply in the issue of environmental governance, as seen in the Amazon in Brazil where corporate and community interests have been fought through legal processes. However, there are many contradictions in how sovereignty applies across local and global commons. In the case of the Amazon, it is highlighted that host sovereignty means that collectively "an area the size of Wales"[4] in the UK is permitted to disappear every year. This loss of land is leading to violations of the rights of Indigenous people and other forest dwellers whose livelihoods depend on living in the Amazon and its conservation (Adelman, 2019). Repair can be through democratic transformation (De Greiff, 2006) where outcomes for justice can be improved by steps towards reclaiming sovereignty.

[4] The size of Wales is estimated to be 2,122,400 hectares and a rugby pitch is estimated to be one hectare in size for comparison. BBC, 2019 (see: https://www.bbc.co.uk/news/uk-wales-46737277).

6 Responsibility-Sharing and Financing

The overlapping growth and development paradigms that have been discussed are central to understanding the lack of progress towards decarbonisation. A recognition of planetary boundaries and the need to transition, due to the risk of a global systemic collapse is at the forefront of environmental and development agendas (IPCC, 2023). As has been recognised, a powerful set of countries account for most carbon emissions, the ongoing ecological colonialism of fossil fuel industries, extraction, and deforestation. However, their culpability is still under-acknowledged in shaping policy options and responses for climate mitigation and adaptation. Although a huge amount of financial transfer is needed for this climate adaptation, almost 70 per cent of international climate financing is taking the form of debt-creating loans (UNCTAD, 2024). Countries cannot be expected to finance their adaptation when countries rich from colonialism have caused much of the damage that they are exposed to, with many risks to lives every year as countries experience extreme weather conditions.

In efforts to both decarbonise and decolonise the question becomes how to ensure climate adaptation and avert ecological crises, using instruments other than debt. The need for moving beyond climate and anthropocentric analysis to consider ecological imperialism becomes highly relevant (Crosby, 1986/2009). It was significant that in UN Framework Convention on Climate Change discussions in 2021, a loss and damage fund was set up, using principles of reparations introduced by Bolivia into this dialogue in 2009 (Guterres, 2023). Climate devastation has been caused, in significant part, by the industrialisation of powerful countries (Worley et al., 2022), thus the responsibility for financing for climate mitigation lies within the framing of a polluter pays model (Kim, 2023).

7 Conclusion

This discussion extends a challenge for decarbonisation to reconcile ongoing coloniality, arguing this can be achieved through reparative justice. The origins of global wealth from colonial extraction and drain have not been fully acknowledged, and the harm it caused through the reign of empires remains unremedied. This colonial drain is the root cause of poverty and climate injustice. A holistic approach requires moving beyond treating decarbonisation challenges as a matter of getting the right modality of policies and means using decolonial approaches as a moral anchor towards justice of distribution. In this chapter policies such as redistribution to curb the growing concentration of wealth are referenced, as well as the closing tax evasion loopholes to stop avoidance by multinational corporations as another legacy of economic coloniality. This could make more fiscal space available for climate adaptation. Moving from decarbonisation to climate justice also requires the unsettling of processes of knowledge production that inform policy development towards a much stronger informed approach on repair conceptualities and their value.

References

Acemoglu, D., & Robinson, J. A. (2000). Why did the west extend the franchise? Democracy, inequality, and growth in historical perspective. *The Quarterly Journal of Economics, 115*(4), 1167–1199. https://doi.org/10.1162/003355300555042. Accessed 15 May 2025.

Adelman, S. (2019). *Sovereignty or sustainability in the Anthropocene*. University of Warwick. https://wrap.warwick.ac.uk/id/eprint/110583/2/WRAP-sovereignty-sustainability-anthropocene-Adelman-2018.pdf. Accessed 15 May 2025.

Adelman, S. (2020). Beyond development: Towards sustainability and climate justice in the Anthropocene. In *The limits of law and development* (pp. 54–72). Routledge.

Bhambra, G. K. (2022). A decolonial project for Europe. *JCMS: Journal of Common Market Studies, 60*(2), 229–244.

Brissett, N. O. (2025). Delinking development: Material and epistemic justice and Caribbean reparations. In *Transforming development in education* (pp. 113–137). Edward Elgar Publishing. https://www.elgaronline.com/downloadpdf/edcollchap-oa/book/9781035337798/chapter6.pdf. Accessed 15 May 2025.

Carbon Brief. (2021). *Analysis. Which countries are historically responsible for climate change*? https://www.carbonbrief.org/analysis-which-countries-are-historically-responsible-for-climate-change/. Accessed 15 May 2025.

Chancel, L., Piketty, T., Saez, E., & Zucman, G. (Eds.) (2022). *World inequality report 2022*. Harvard University Press. https://books.google.com/books?hl=en&lr=&id=DN-VEAAAQBAJ&oi=fnd&pg=PA2&dq=Chancel+and+Piketty. Accessed 15 May 2025.

Chinweizu, I. (1993, April). Reparations and a new global order: A comparative overview. In *A paper read at the second plenary session of the first pan-African conference on reparations, Abuja, Nigeria* (Vol. 27).

Cushion, S. (2021). Decolonising and decarbonising. *International Union Rights, 28*(3), 5–6. https://muse.jhu.edu/pub/438/article/845099/summary. Accessed 15 May 2025.

Danewid, I. (2020). The fire this time: Grenfell, racial capitalism and the urbanisation of empire. *European Journal of International Relations, 26*(1), 289–313.

Darity, W. A., Jr., & Mullen, A. K. (2020). *From here to equality: Reparations for black Americans in the twenty-first century*. The University of North Carolina Press.

Darity, W., Jr., Mullen, A. K., & Slaughter, M. (2022). The cumulative costs of racism and the bill for black reparations. *Journal of Economic Perspectives, 36*(2), 99–122.

Davis, P., & Sanchez-Martinez, M. (2015). *Economic theories of poverty*. Joseph Rowntree Foundation.

de Sousa Santos, B. (2021). Postcolonialism, decoloniality, and epistemologies of the south. In *Oxford research Encyclopedia of literature*. https://doi.org/10.1093/acrefore/9780190201098.001.0001/acrefore-9780190201098-e-1262

Delfin, A. (2025). *Public debt: A Southern Perspective—Asian Peoples' Movement on Debt and Development (APMDD)* [online] Asian Peoples' Movement on Debt and Development (APMDD). Available at: https://apmdd.org/public-debt-a-southern-perspective/. Accessed 15 May 2025.

Donaghy, T. Q., Healy, N., Jiang, C. Y., et al. (2023). Fossil fuel racism in the United States: How phasing out coal, oil, and gas can protect communities. *Energy Research and Social Science, 100*, Article 103104. https://doi.org/10.1016/j.erss.2023.103104

Dymski, G. (2021). Intersectional inequality and global economic power: Self-feeding dynamics within and across national borders. *International Journal of Political Economy, 50*(3), 189–197.

Fanon, F. (1961). *The wretched of the earth*. Grove Press.

Friedlingstein, P., et al. (2024). *Global carbon budget 2024*. https://eprints.whiterose.ac.uk/170047/1/essd-12-3269-2020.pdf. Accessed 15 May 2025.

Gattey, E. (2021). Global histories of empire and climate in the Anthropocene. *History Compass, 19*(8), Article e12683.

Grasso, M. (2024). The case for climate reparations by fossil fuel companies: Ethical foundations, monetary estimates and feasibility. *Development and Change, 55*(4), 727–751. https://doi.org/10.1111/dech.12837

De Greiff, P. (2006). Justice and reparations. *The handbook of reparations, 451*. Retrieved March 26, 2025, from https://scholar.archive.org/work/sntrav5vuvgrvj5uixjaimttxm/access/wayback/http://www.queensu.ca:80/conferences/reparations/papers/De%20Greiff%20paper.pdf. Accessed 15 May 2025.

Grenfell Action Group. (2016). *KCTMO—Playing with fire!* Available at: https://grenfellactiongroup.wordpress.com/2016/11/20/kctmo-playing-with-fire/. Accessed 15 May 2025.

Griffin, A. (2017). Grenfell Tower cladding that may have led to fire was chosen to improve appearance of Kensington block of flats. *The Independent*. Available at: http://www.independent.co.uk/news/uk/home-news/grenfell-tower-cladding-fire-cause-improve-kensington-block-flats-appearance-blaze-24-storey-west-a7789951.html. Accessed 15 May 2025.

Guterres, A. (2023). The Era of Global Boiling Has Arrived. *says UN chief as July set to be hottest month on record| Climate science| The Guardian.*

Hickel, J., 2020. *Less is more: How degrowth will save the world*. Random House.

IPCC. (2023). Climate change 2023: Synthesis report, summary for policymakers. In Core Writing Team, H. Lee, and J. Romero (Eds.), *Contribution of working groups I, II and III to the sixth assessment report of the intergovernmental panel on climate change*. IPCC, Geneva, Switzerland. https://mural.maynoothuniversity.ie/17886/1/IPCC_AR6_SYR_SPM.pdf. Accessed 15 May 2025.

Karenga, M. (2022). *The ethical imperative of Serudj Ta: To repair, renew and remake the world*. https://ibw21.org/commentary/dr-maulana-karenga/the-ethical-imperative-of-serudj-ta/. Accessed 15 May 2025.

Kim, H. (2023). Structural transformation and reparative obligation: Reinterpreting the beneficiary pays principle. *Journal of Social Philosophy*. https://doi.org/10.1111/josp.12524

Konczal, M., Milani, K., & Evans, A. (2022). *The empirical failures of neoliberalism*. https://rooseveltinstitute.org/wp-content/uploads/2020/07/RI_The-Empirical-Failures-of-Neoliberalism_brief-202001.pdf. Accessed 15 May 2025.

Koram, K. (2022). The legalization of cannabis and the question of reparations. *Journal of International Economic Law*, *25*(2), 294–311. https://academic.oup.com/jiel/article-pdf/25/2/294/45293536/jgac026.pdf. Accessed 15 May 2025.

Koshy, S., Cacho, L. M., Byrd, J., & Jefferson, B. J. (Eds.). (2022). *Colonial racial capitalism*. Duke University Press.

Kothari, U., 2006. An agenda for thinking about 'race' in development. *Progress in development studies, 6*(1), pp. 9–23.

Kundnani, A. (2023). *What is antiracism? And why it means anticapitalism*. Verso Books. Available at: https://books.google.com/books?hl=en&lr=&id=sNJ3EAAAQBAJ&oi=fnd&pg=PA1&dq=Kundnani. Accessed 15 May 2025.

Lahiri, B. and Darity Jr, W.A. (2024). Global North–South Reparations: Demand-side and Supply-side Policies with a Dynamic View of International Trade and Finance. *Development and Change, 55*(4), pp. 672–699.

LankaWeb. (2023). *Climate colonialism at CoP 28: Carbon Laundering via Green Bondscams*? Lankaweb.com. https://www.lankaweb.com/news/items/2023/12/02/climate-colonialism-at-cop-28-carbon-laundering-via-green-bondscams/. Accessed 15 May 2025.

Lapavitsas, C., & Soydan, A. (2022). Financialisation in developing countries: approaches, concepts, and metrics. *International Review of Applied Economics, 36*(3), 424–447. https://doi.org/10.1080/02692171.2022.2052714

Lapola, D. M., Pinho, P., Barlow, J., Aragão, L. E., Berenguer, E., Carmenta, R., Liddy, H. M., Seixas, H., Silva, C. V., Silva-Junior, C. H., & Alencar, A. A. (2023). The drivers and impacts of Amazon forest degradation. *Science, 379*(6630), eabp8622.

Longley, R. (2021). *What is colonialism? Definition and examples*. ThoughtCo. https://www.thoughtco.com/colonialism-definition-and-examples-5112779. Accessed 15 May 2025.

Macklem, P. (2005). Rybna 9, Praha 1: Restitution and memory in international human rights law. *European Journal of International Law, 16*(1), 1–23.

Martin, G. (1985). The historical, economic, and political bases of France's African policy. *The Journal of Modern African Studies, 23*(2), 189–208. https://doi.org/10.1017/s0022278x00000148

Mercer, H., & Simpson, T. (2023). Imperialism, colonialism, and climate change science. *Wiley Interdisciplinary Reviews Climate Change*. https://doi.org/10.1002/wcc.851

Mignolo, W. (2007). Delinking: The rhetoric of modernity, the logic of coloniality and the grammar of de-coloniality. *Cultural Studies, 21*(2), 449–514.

Muchhala, B. (2022). *The structural power of the state-finance nexus: Systemic delinking for the right to development*. Society for International Development.

Narayanaswamy, L., Efange, S., & Woodroffe, J. (2021). *Decolonising aid*. Gender and Development Network. https://static1.squarespace.com/static/536c4ee8e4b0b60bc6ca7c74/t/60ef2c1f33c2d110098feca5/1626287136282/Decolonising+Aid-+Briefing+.pdf. Accessed 15 May 2025.

Obeng-Odoom, F. (2023). Ecological reparations. In *Handbook on alternative global development* (pp. 352–361). Edward Elgar Publishing.

Osofisan, W. (2020). *Opinion: Why the black lives matter movement should have us rethinking humanitarian aid*. Devex Blog. See: https://www.devex.com/news/opinion-why-the-black-lives-matter-movement-should-have-us-rethinking-humanitarian-aid-98570. Accessed 15 May 2025.

Otele, O. (2009). British slavers against abolition. *Revue Francaise de Civilisation Britannique, 15*(1), 161–175. https://crecib.org/wp-content/uploads/2017/04/05volxvn1otele.pdf. Accessed 15 May 2025.

Oxfam. (2024). Inequality Inc. How corporate power divides our world and the need for a new ear of public action. https://www.oxfamnovib.nl/Files/rapporten/2024/bp-inequality-inc-150124-eng-embargoed.pdf. Accessed 15 May 2025.

Patnaik, P. (2015). Capitalism and inequality. *Agrarian South: Journal of Political Economy, 4*(2), pp. 153–168.

Patnaik, U., & Patnaik, P. (2021). *"The Neoliberal Regime." Capital and Imperialism, Theory, History and the Present*, pp. 267–83.

Paulson, S. (2024). World-making technology entangled with coloniality, race and gender: Ecomodernist and degrowth perspectives. *Environmental Values, 33*(1), 71–89.

Perkins, P. E. E. (2019). Climate justice, commons, and degrowth. *Ecological Economics, 160*, 183–190.

Perry, K. K. (2021). The new 'bond-age', climate crisis and the case for climate reparations: Unpicking old/new colonialities of finance for development within the SDGs. *Geoforum, 126*, 361–371. https://osf.io/preprints/socarxiv/h9s2z/download. Accessed 15 May 2025.

Pieratos, N., & Two Bulls, K. (2021). *Landback: A necessary act of reparations*. https://nonprofitquarterly.org/wp-content/uploads/2021/10/2802_Summer_2021_Pieratos_Two_Bulls.pdf. Accessed 15 May 2025.

Prashad, V. (2007). *The darker nations: A people's history of the third world*. The New Press.

Richardson, K., et al. (2023). Earth beyond six of nine planetary boundaries. *Science Advances*. https://doi.org/10.1126/sciadv.adh2458

Ringmar, E. (2019). *History of international relations: A non-European perspective* (p. 232). Open Book Publishers. https://library.oapen.org/bitstream/handle/20.500.12657/24805/1/9781783740246.pdf. Accessed 15 May 2025.

Shelton, R. E., & Eakin, H. (2022). Who's fighting for justice? Advocacy in energy justice and just transition scholarship. *Environmental Research Letters, 17*(6), Article 063006.

Smith, J. (2016). *All roads lead into the crisis in imperialism in the twenty-first century, globalization, super-exploitation, and capitalism's final crisis* (pp. 279–319). Monthly Review Press.

Stevis, D., & Felli, R. (2015). Global labour unions and just transition to a green economy. *International Environmental Agreements: Politics, Law and Economics, 15*, 29–43.

Stockholm Resilience Centre. (n.d.). *Planetary boundaries*. https://www.stockholmresilience.org/research/planetary-boundaries.html. Accessed 15 May 2025.

Sultana, F. (2022). Critical climate justice. *The Geographical Journal, 188*(1), 118–124.

Sumner, A., et al. (2021). Measuring global poverty before and during the pandemic: A political economy of overoptimism. *Third World Quarterly, 43*(1), 1–17. https://doi.org/10.1080/01436597.2021.1995712

Táíwò, O. O. (2022). *Reconsidering reparations*. Oxford University Press. Available at: https://books.google.com/books?hl=en&lr=&id=7fdQEAAAQBAJ&oi=fnd&pg=PP1&dq=Táíwò. Accessed 15 May 2025.

The Guardian. (2018). *Natives: Race and class in the ruins of empire by Akala—Review* [online] Available at: https://www.theguardian.com/books/2018/may/20/natives-akala-review-destroying-myths-of-race-afia-hirsch. Accessed 15 May 2025.

UN DESA. (2022). UN DESA Policy Brief No. 144: Moving Beyond GDP and Achieving Our Common Agenda with Natural Capital Accounting. https://desapublications.un.org/policy-briefs/un-desa-policy-brief-no-144-moving-beyond-gdp-and-achieving-our-common-agenda-natural. Accessed 15 May 2025.

UN News. (2024). *Accelerating extinction rate triggers domino effect of biodiversity loss*. https://news.un.org/en/story/2024/05/1150056. Accessed 15 May 2025.

UN Resolution A/76/L.75. (2022). *The human right to a clean, healthy and sustainable environment*. https://digitallibrary.un.org/record/3982508?ln=en&v=pdf. Accessed 15 May 2025.

United Nations Conference on Trade and Development (UNCTAD). (2024). *A world of debt report 2024*.

Upham, P., Sovacool, B., & Ghosh, B. (2022). Just transitions for industrial decarbonisation: A framework for innovation, participation, and justice. *Renewable and Sustainable Energy Reviews, 167*, 112699. https://www.sciencedirect.com/science/article/pii/S1364032122005883. Accessed 15 May 2025.

Wimbadi, R. W., & Djalante, R. (2020). From decarbonization to low carbon development and transition: A systematic literature review of the conceptualization of moving toward net-zero carbon dioxide emission (1995–2019). *Journal of Cleaner Production, 256*(2020), Article 120307. https://doi.org/10.1016/j.jclepro.2020.120307

World Bank. (2021). *Blog: Global wealth has grown but at the expense of future prosperity*. https://www.worldbank.org/en/news/press-release/2021/10/27/global-wealth-has-grown-but-at-the-expense-of-future-prosperity-world-bank. Accessed 15 May 2025.

World Bank. (2022). *World development indicators*. GDP growth (annual %), World, 2014–2022.

Worley, W., & Jerving, S. (2022). *Mia Mottley Hints at G-7 Support for the Bridgetown Agenda at COP 27*, Devex, 7 Nov. 2022. https://www.devex.com/news/mia-mottley-hints-at-g-7-support-for-the-bridgetown-agenda-at-cop-27-104387. Accessed 15 May 2025.

Zajontz, T. (2022). Debt, distress, dispossession: Towards a critical political economy of Africa's financial dependency. *Review of African Political Economy, 49*(171), 173–183.

Climate Change, Economics, and the Global South: A Case of a Triplet Crisis

Ying Chen and Yannis Bougiatiotis

Abstract The acute climate crisis, the failure of the Economics' discipline to analyze and respond to the climate emergency, and the complex environmental and developmental challenges of the Global South constitute an interconnected triplet crisis. This chapter critically explores a wide set of contending discourses such as neoclassical Environmental Economics, Ecological Economics, Post-Growth, De-Growth Approaches as well as Marxist and Post-Colonial/Post-Development frameworks. This exploration underscores the methodological flaws as well as the North-Centric approach of the dominant neoclassical approach which has led to the exacerbation of the climate crisis and the under-recognition of the crisis of the Global South. While critical perspectives, such as Ecological Economics, Post-growth and De-growth, constitute responses to the analytical crisis of mainstream economics, they often offer a vague analysis of capitalism's role in driving the climate crisis and overlook the complex challenges of the Global South under the hierarchical global divisions

Y. Chen (✉) · Y. Bougiatiotis
Department of Economics, The New School for Social Research, New York, USA
e-mail: yingc@newschool.edu

Y. Bougiatiotis
e-mail: bougi087@newschool.edu

A. Agunsoye and A. Arntsen (eds.), *Decarbonising and Decolonising Economics*, https://doi.org/10.1007/978-3-032-11972-8_3

of economic and political power. By recognizing these limitations, the chapter contends that the interconnectedness of the triplet crisis is best understood by the frameworks of ecological colonialism and ecological imperialism. Despite their analytical differences, both frameworks provide crucial insights neglected by both mainstream economics and many of its critics and constitute a solid initial step for the decarbonization and decolonization of the economics discipline.

Keywords Ecological colonialism · Ecological imperialism · Climate change · Economic theoretical frameworks

1 Introduction

The severity of the current climate crisis is evident in the fact that global temperatures are already shooting through the 1.5 °C threshold above pre-industrial levels set by the Paris Agreement (World Meteorological Organization, 2025). Yet, the discipline of economics has struggled to adequately address key features of this capitalistically induced environmental derailment leading to the ongoing ecological destruction of today. Meanwhile, the Global South faces unprecedented economic and environmental challenges. Decades of uneven development have deepened socio-economic inequalities and widened the human development gap (UNDP, 2024). On the ecological front, societies of the Global South are severely impacted by rising temperatures and increasingly frequent extreme weather events like floods, sea-level rise, and droughts. These events lead to both voluntary and involuntary patterns of mobility, displacement, and immobility among the communities of the Global South (Almuhil et al., 2024). Furthermore, the natural disasters of the current climate emergency are largely responsible for high mortality rates and significant economic costs for the Global South (World Meteorological Association, 2023).[1] Overall, the crisis of climate, the economics

[1] Between 1970 and 2012, the economic costs from disasters attributed to weather, climate and water extremes are calculated at US$ 43 billion for Africa, US$ 1.4 trillion for Asia and US$ 115.2 billion for South America (World Meteorological Organization, 2023).

discipline, and the development and environmental challenges of the Global South form an interconnected "triplet crisis".

This chapter explores the plurality of theoretical frameworks that seek to understand and respond to climate change. The main aim is to uncover the core misunderstandings surrounding climate change and the failure of mainstream but also many critical economics frameworks to recognize and act decisively to this triplet crisis. It should be noted that economics is not the only discipline that seeks to understand the roots and impacts of climate change but, nonetheless, it holds hegemonic power over other disciplines, professional studies, and policy-making.

Through the examination of the various theoretical frameworks, we contend that the dominant mainstream framework of neoclassical environmental economics has important methodological flaws and, similarly to the critical ecological Economics approach, suffers from Eurocentric bias. Furthermore, by exploring early and late critiques of the growth imperative of Neoclassical Economics, the chapter argues that these approaches offer a vague analysis of capitalism's role in the climate crisis and overlook the complex environmental and development challenges faced by the Global South. The only frameworks that engage holistically with the triplet crisis are those of ecological imperialism and ecological colonialism. Despite their analytical differences, they question many core features of both mainstream and critical frameworks over climate change. By means of conclusion, the chapter maintains that the recognition and response to the triplet crisis runs through the decolonizing and decarbonizing of the economics discipline and its understanding of climate change.

2 Climate Change Through the Lens of Mainstream Economics

In 2018, Yale economist William D. Nordhaus won the Nobel Memorial Prize in Economic Sciences "for integrating climate change into long-run macroeconomic analysis" (Royal Swedish Academy of Sciences, 2018, para 1). Given the dominance of the mainstream approach in economics, it is not surprising that pioneering work of Neoclassical Economics on climate change was eventually awarded with a Nobel Prize. In contrast to the euphoria among the mainstream camp, many climate scholars and activists coined Nordhaus' success as a "climate catastrophe" (Hickel, 2018). While his work on climate economics is considered notable in the economics discipline, it is methodologically ridden by the misconceptions of the mainstream approach and partly responsible for a long period of policy inaction that has contributed to the severe climate crisis of our time.

The three cornerstones of neoclassical economics are no other than preferences, technology and endowments of individual actors. In the most elementary form, hyper-rational individuals are optimizing their utility under conditions of scarcity of endowments and given technological constraints, which in mathematical parlance translates to the point where marginal benefit is equal to marginal cost (Varian, 1992, p. 100). Essential to this process of "calculation" is the controversial quantification of the subjective utility individual consumers experience via consumption as well as the value of nature. Nordhaus (1977, p. 55) uses this cost–benefit analysis framework in his seminal work and advocates as a rational choice the postponement of carbon-reducing climate actions for at least twenty more years. As he explicitly mentions,

> according to the cost schedules assumed in the model, it does not pay to curtail carbondioxide emissions until nearly the time when the limit is reached; and for the three cases examined this time comes in the 1990–2010 period or the 2010–2030 period [...] for it implies that there is still a comfortable amount of time to continue research and to consider plans for implementation of carbon dioxide control if it is deemed necessary (Nordhaus, 1977, p. 55).

In another influential paper, Nordhaus (1991) uses the features of the US economy as the reference point in forecasting the world economy 60 years into the future. Based on this assumption, he further presumes that climate change would adversely impact only a few sectors of the economy. More specifically, the paper argues that the effects of climate change would be contained only to the agricultural sector while heavy industry sectors, such as manufacturing and mining, as well as service and trade sectors would only suffer "negligible effects". Based on this second assumption, Nordhaus contends that only 3% of the US output comes from highly sensitive sectors to climate change. To bring his argument into closure, he calculates the damage of climate change to world GNP in 2050, using the composition of US GNP in 1981 as representative for the entire world in 2050 (Nordhaus, 1991, p. 930). His often-cited conclusion is that even with a 3 °C rise in global mean temperature since the time of measurement (1.5°C above the Paris Agreement's primary goal), the negative impact on the *level* of GDP will be about only 0.25–2%, which is almost a negligible impact given that the measure of the impact is the *level* of, rather than the *growth rate* of, GDP (Keen, 2021).[2]

Notwithstanding, Nordhaus' assumptions echo a North-centric modernization approach (Rostow 1960), according to which the US is the reference of development for the entire world. Such an aggregate approach abstracts from the existing heterogeneities in the global division of labor between the Global North and the Global South. Furthermore, even mainstream analyses regarding the impact of weather variability underscore the major disruptions of the supply chains across sectors (Quante et al., 2024). Nordhaus' claim about the sensitivity of sectors and the sectoral composition is thus erroneous. In reality, we should therefore expect greater than estimated damages to global income by climate change and, given the existing structural productive asymmetries between Global North and Global South, also disproportionately more significant damages on the more vulnerable developing economies (Quante et al., 2024).

Nordhaus' work not only dominated theoretical understanding but also impacted profoundly policymaking. For example, the 2014 IPCC (Intergovernmental Panel on Climate Change) report, a source of reference for global policymaking, still drew from conclusions found in Nordhaus' work regarding the negligible estimates of global economic damages (IPCC, 2014; Keen, 2021). The conclusions of the report aligned with his previous reassuring estimations, arguing that "for most economic sectors, the impact of climate change will be small relative to the impacts of other drivers…", referring to population change, technological advancement, income fluctuations, etc. as "other drivers" (IPCC, 2014, p. 622).

Since uncertainty prevails, the IPCC 2014 report is far from optimistic regarding the economic impact of climate change. There are repeated alarms throughout the report relating to the existence of many unknowns. Examples in the report include the lack of full understanding of the

[2] If a country's GDP is 1000 billion USD in year 1, then a 2% negative impact on the level of GDP means that GDP will shrink by 2% in year 2, amounting to 980 billion USD. However, if the previous annual GDP growth rate is 1%, then a 2-percentage point negative impact on the growth rate could result in −1% GDP growth and a recession.

magnitude of the potential adverse impact of climate change to "productivity and economic growth" as well as the yet unclear economic implications of climate change for "water supply infrastructure" (IPCC, 2014, p. 663). Despite the acknowledgment of many uncertainties, mainstream economics and the policy world, as indicated in this section, opt for straightforward and simplistic solutions to climate change over complicated and structural ones, a tendency which self-enforces treating the climate crisis simplistically and advocating for "elementary" answers such as finding the correct pricing for carbon. In this connection, it is not hard to understand why Nordhaus' description of a distorted yet simplistic certainty, versus a complex and intimidating uncertainty, gained traction in the policy world. The policy choice of hegemonic powers, such as the US, to delay action under conditions of uncertainty had negatively impacted and is still adversely impacting hundreds of millions of people around the world, both located in the Global North and the Global South.

Post-festum, scholars have updated the assumptions of Nordhaus' original model. The previous conclusion that a 3.5 °C of warming by 2100 might be an economically desirable outcome is now revised to below 2 °C (Hänsel et al., 2020). Exactly as global capitalism is already shooting beyond these targets, the decades of policy inactions and the resulting ecological damages loom large over the failure to contain and address the climate crisis. Very few mainstream economists are willing to openly acknowledge the fact that economic measures are never adequate to address the enormous uncertainties of climate change. Even if they do, they tend to filter out the limits of their assumptions about unprecedented structural uncertainties and selectively present the inadequate measures as clear-cut answers which are then adopted by practitioners who have "a low level of tolerance for vagueness" and "little place for even a whiff of fuzziness" (see Weitzman, 2011, p. 289). Overall, the failure of mainstream economics to meaningfully theorize and battle climate change is 'hard evidence' about the interconnectedness of the crisis of the environment and the economics discipline.

3 Ecological Economics and their Critique of Environmental Economics

Nordhaus is by no means the only renowned neoclassical economist whose work contributes to the decades-long policy inactions towards climate change. Another Economics Nobel Laureate, Kenneth Arrow, together with a group of ecologists and economists also addressed the question of excessive consumption and sustainability on the basis of two criteria (Arrow et al., 2004).

The first is the standard neoclassical criterion of utility maximization, with future utility all discounted into present values, which implies a subjective assessment of how much human beings today value the welfare of their future generation. According to this criterion, "actual consumption today is excessive if it is greater than the level of current consumption prescribed by this optimal consumption path... current consumption is excessive if lowering it and increasing investment (or reducing disinvestment) in capital assets could raise future utility enough to more than compensate (even after discounting) for the loss in current utility" (Arrow et al., 2004, p. 149). In simpler terms, if a reduction of consumption today and a corresponding increase in investment can provide a level of future utility high enough to outweigh the sacrifice of present for future consumption then current consumption is considered excessive. This explanation suggests the comparison for consumption level is relative to investment level, and that the ultimate goal of this comparison is maximization of inter-temporal utility.

The second criterion is sustainability, which refers to "the ability of the economy to maintain living standards", translated into the mathematical expression according to which "the intertemporal social welfare V must not decrease over time". In other words, the criterion is that the future generation's utility does not decline over time, which is consistent with the definition of sustainable development, which refers to "development that meets the needs of the present without compromising the ability of future generations to meet their own needs" (Arrow et al., 2004, p. 150).

The conclusion of the paper is that all the countries under examination, rich or poor, have exhibited the "excessive consumption" pattern, meaning that the "consumption share of the output is higher than..." the optimal consumption level that maximizes the intertemporal utility. However, the article emphasized that it does not mean that the poor nations were also over-consuming in the conventional sense. Rather, the results can only suggest that the poor countries were under-investing since both the investment and consumption levels in the poor countries are too low. Yet, Arrow et al. (2004, p. 166) and his colleagues recognized the limits of their measure by acknowledging the connection between high levels of consumption in rich countries and excessive resource degradation in poor ones.

To this approach, Ecological Economics' reaction was that the neoclassical economists were asking the wrong question. Instead of assessing whether the consumption is excess (relative to investment), the more important and urgent question should be what is the "optimal scale of macroeconomy relative to biosphere", which is not a question acknowledged by mainstream neoclassical economics (Daly et al., 2007). Ecological Economics has emerged as an alternative to the orthodoxy of Environmental Economics—as discussed in Sect. 2—(Morgan & Daly, 2019) and focuses on two core aspects: the limits of the ecosystem and the economy as "an open subsystem of a larger ecosystem that is finite, non-growing, and materially closed (though open with respect to solar energy)" (Daily, 2015). In contrast to the neoclassical-influenced Environmental Economics, Ecological Economics reject the possibility of unlimited GDP growth and instead maintain that there is "an optimal scale beyond which physical growth in the economic subsystem begins to reduce total welfare by diminishing the sources of ecological services faster than it increases the sources of production services" (Morgan & Daly, 2019, p. 139).

The framework of Ecological Economics questions the utilitarian foundations of neoclassical economics and its most fundamental assumptions. With respect to utility maximization, the very concept of utility is subjective to each individual and thus inherently cannot be quantified. Since "utility is an experience, not a material thing" without a "natural" growth of rate (Daly et al., 2007, p. 1360), the central place of discounting future quantities into the present (Hänsel et al., 2020) is unjustifiable and utility itself a meaningless and risky guide to determining, let alone addressing, the limits of the natural and material world. As far as the core assumptions are concerned, Ecological Economics challenge the assumption of substitutability of produced and natural goods. To the extent that the consumption of produced goods necessitates the existence of natural goods (i.e. diving gears—coral reefs and hiking books—natural trails), natural goods are complementary to produced ones (Daly et al.,

2007). The rejection of the substitutability assumption thus leads to the questioning of its use as a solution to natural resource scarcity.

Instead, the framework emphasizes the ecological limits of the natural world and rejects growthism in both Neoclassical and Keynesian frameworks. (Daly, 2015, p. 9). To address these limits, Ecological Economics highlights the importance of limiting "scale or physical size of the economy relative to the containing ecosystem" and advocates for a steady-state economy. In a steady-state economy population and capital stock do not grow more, although "the art of living would continue to improve" (Daly, 2015, p. 11). In today's context, equality of birth and death rates as well as production and depreciation rates characterize the economy. Steady-state can come about by either a high-level or low-level equilibrium. In the former case, society will experience both high fertility and mortality rates and from the perspective of consumption, high rates will predominate in societies with excessive consumerism and wasting. In the latter case, the birth and death rates will converge in societies with longevity yet low fertility, and similarly durability in the realm of consumption goods. It is the second low-rate equilibrium which is the ideal steady-state for Ecological Economics.

What becomes evident is the lack of recognition of the position of the Global South in the steady-state framework. For ecological economists such as Daly, population control is essential for a steady-state economy, and especially a low birth rate matched by equally low death rates, a society of mature population with reduced fertility (Morgan & Daly, 2019). Yet the picture in the Global South, and particularly the poorer countries, is radically different. Poverty is associated with limited access to social services and low life expectancy and high levels of fertility. Population control policies, advocated by steady-state frameworks, will unavoidably have to aim at poor countries which in turn raises concerns for its Malthusian and racist implications (Chen, 2023). On the whole, although Ecological Economics provides a solid critique to the reasoning of mainstream Economics over climate change, its visions appear to have overlooked the realities of the Global South.

4 Early and Late Critiques of the Role of Growth on Climate Crisis

Critiques of the consumption bias heralded in neoclassical economics as well as the socio-ecological impacts of the growth imperative came from various fronts within and outside mainstream thinking. One of the early reactions to the imperative of growth, the role of consumption, and the impact of the scale of production on nature and society came from Schumacher. Although not an ecological thinker per se (Singh, 2023) and highly idiosyncratic[3] with respect to his theoretical influences, Schumacher's (1973) idea of "*Small is beautiful*" became a popular critique of mainstream thinking around issues of ecological sustainability and sustainable development (Toye, 2012; Binns, 2006, pp. 218–222).

Schumacher staunchly critiqued the so-called "subjectivity" of economics and the "impartiality" of numbers. He argued that the quantitative measurement of GDP without contemplating the qualitative dimensions of its components (such as the depletion of natural resources) led to distorted visions of prosperity. The "materialist philosophy of over-production and over-consumption" led to ever-increasing demands on a world of finite resources and elevated higher consumption to the absolute standard of well-being (Schumacher, 1973). Identifying the big scale economic and social structures as impersonal, insensitive, and power-driven, Schumacher promoted the small scale as "free, efficient, creative, enjoyable and enduring" (Varma, 2003, 1), in his words, the "small as beautiful". The rural sector encapsulated the values of small while the urban and industrial scale the principles of large—the duality created by the rise of the latter worked in the detriment to the values of the former (Varma, 2003). Schumacher emphasized that mechanization and industrial techniques, associated with "traditional" industrialization, exacerbated the intensive use of non-renewable resources and the exhaustion

[3] Schumacher's analytical lens is shaped by a wide and contradictory group of thinkers such as Keynes, Marx and Gandhi and is deeply influenced by the ideas of liberation, simplicity, anti- consumption and non-violence found in Buddhist economics (Binns 2006; Toye 2012; Varma 2003). Schumacher shares the emphasis of the Keynesian tradition on full-employment, recognizes Marx's critique on the negative impacts of capitalist society on the "quality of life" and follows Gandhi's critique of mass production and Western modernization. His work particularly echoes the Buddhist emphasis on the priority of the spiritual over the material, the wastefulness of natural resources as violence, and less consumption as means of well-being.

of world natural reserves (Singh, 2023, 8), creating thus forms of ecological violence particularly for future generations. The industrial large-scale technologies only led to the deepening of the social and environmental crisis.

Schumacher identified solutions to what he considered the environmental and human predicaments of gigantism predominantly in the sphere of the type and scale of technologies (Toye, 2012). The choice over technology became pivotal for Schumacher's thought over development policies of "poor countries" (McRobie, 1974, 221) as he argued against them importing capital-intensive and non-renewable resource intensive technologies from rich countries and in favor of intermediate- and small-scale technologies combining traditional and modern techniques (Toye, 2012; Varma, 2003). Intermediate technologies would promote harmony with people and the environment and depend less on non-renewable resources (McRobie, 1981: 1). Such "technologies with a human face" would prioritize the principle of non-violence respecting "ecological limits" and working symbiotically with nature (McRobie, 1974, 218); sustainability was to be found on the small "*human scale*". McRobie (1981), then Chairman of the Intermediate Technology Development Group, presented a wide set of examples of human scale technologies spanning from agriculture to energy such as plows, screw press for sugar extraction to windmills for local manufacturing and river turbines.

Schumacher's ideas had a significant impact on the debates of growth and its socio-ecological implications. Notwithstanding, Schumacher's opposition to the negative environmental and social *consequences* of large-scale technologies led him to fetishize the small scale and romanticize the agrarian work and rural world (Singh, 2023) advocating the primacy of a "technical fix" over a "social fix" to the non-sustainability of "mainstream" growth (Varma, 2003, 5). As discussed in the remainder of this section, these early critiques of Schumacher remain relevant to contemporary frameworks that, in one way or another, incorporate versions of "small is beautiful".

Many of Schumacher's arguments were echoed in de-growth and post-growth who emerged since the 2000s, placing primary emphasis on the critique of GDP growth. In contrast to Schumacher who, albeit the weaknesses of his argument, included the perspective of developing economies in his critique, the debates between these two approaches are largely constrained within the boundaries of advanced capitalism's politics, and thus unable to acknowledge the development challenges of the Global South and its possible connection with radical anti-capitalist agendas that transcend narrow policy visions.

Steady-state advocates recognize their affinity with de-growth advocates against neoclassical and Keynesian ideology of growthism (Morgan & Daly, 2019). Notwithstanding, ecological economists see de-growth as emerging from activism and thus lacking theoretical grounding and an actionable set of policies (Morgan & Daly, 2019). This may be a fair critique to the early forming of de-growth as a movement, but over time, many scholars have joined the movement, significantly substantiating theoretically the de-growth framework as a whole (Hickel, 2020; Kallis et al., 2018).

A key distinction between these two frameworks, Ecological Economics and degrowth, is their view on capitalism. Proponents of steady-state type of ecological economics—as discussed in Sect. 3—do not argue that specifically capitalism is the problem, as the growth imperative was adopted both in capitalist and socialist economies in the twentieth century (Daly, 2015). Additionally, they are in agreement with the neoclassical view on the inherent allocative efficiency of the market, although they advocate that there are a set of other important factors that the market is called to respond to than merely the efficient allocation of resources. In this regard, the steady-state framework that Daly draws heavily from in his presentation of Ecological Economics dissociates its critique from the particular *modus operandi* of capitalism and hence does not hold a critical stance towards capitalism per se.

The post-growth approach opposes the degrowth movement, most often in an over-generalized fashion, for its overly critical stance towards capitalism and its lack of concrete policy proposals (Likaj et al., 2022). These two aspects lead to a failure of reaching the wider public who seeks for actionable prescriptions. Instead, one of the major concerns of post-growthists is to engage with mainstream politics. According to advocates"talking explicitly about alternatives to capitalism—like arguing for degrowth—is not a good way of making political progress" and thus the post-growth approach "offers a more promising route for a mainstream political and economic discourse" (Likaj et al., 2022, p. 28).

Post-growthism does not hold a uniform stance towards capitalism. Paech (2017, p. 485), for instance, boldly claims that post-growth, like de-growth, will face the similar issue of political feasibility, which leads to the inference that, at the very best, only green growth is suitable on the basis of political feasibility.

Yet, elevating political feasibility to the standard or limit of judgment against growthism is not value-free. On a deeper level, it implicitly accepts that the analytical focus should lay on the politics of advanced capitalism and creates a false and rather restricting dichotomy between advancing proposals of radical but necessary changes and promoting politically "actionable" reform agendas. This is to say, if post-growthism cannot dispense with political feasibility, as Paech (2017) pointed out, then it must also work with the mechanisms of capitalism, which are fundamentally reliant on relentless capital accumulation, i.e., growth.

Certain post-growthists argue that the political feasibility of their low-growth and ecologically sustainable proposals has rapidly increased with the prevalence of secular stagnation in most wealthy countries (Likaj et al., 2022). While this observation might be true, a low-growth or zero-growth model lays in sharp contrast to the political priorities of development, modernization and bettering of material well-being in the Global South. The discussion of such a scenario for developing countries necessitates an open debate of what the alternatives to address poverty and inequality should look like, under what domestic economic structures and global economic architecture, especially since all these aspects will have significant weight in the growth and development of Global South (Chen, 2022).

Further debates between post-growth and de-growth involve the very concept of growth. The former criticize the latter for overly centering on growth itself and instead advocate that neither positive, zero, or negative growth is strictly associated with human well-being (Likaj et al., 2022). Their main concern is "design[ing] an economy to achieve substantive environmental and social goals" and less "whether these result in economic growth or not" (Likaj et al., 2022, p. 26). According to the post-growth approach, priority must be granted to provision of social benefits (such as employment, pensions and public services) independent of growth (Likaj et al., 2022). They additionally propose that the growth-independent employment policies should include, "a sectoral transformation towards a more service-oriented society, a reduction of working hours, a shift in the focus of technological change to resource productivity (through strong eco-taxes, subsidy cuts, cap-and-trade systems), and reduction in dependency on wage income" (Likaj et al., 2022, p. 27; see also Petschow et al., 2020). In other words, their policy discussions do not engage with the associated results of growth or degrowth, and in this way they view their positions as transcending the debate on growthism versus degrowthism.

To be fair, this critique of degrowth is directed more at common interpretations than its actual definitions. For instance, Hickel (2020, p. 11) defines degrowth as "a planned reduction of energy and resource use designed to bring the economy back into balance with the living world in a way that reduces inequality and improves human well-being", while Kallis (2015, p. 1) explicitly highlighted that "degrowth is not synonymous with recession or depression". This emphasis on human well-being rather than GDP growth aligns closely with the post-growth approach.

Many of the policy proposals of post-growthists such as reducing working hours are not original to the extent that they overlap significantly with de-growth (Kallis et al., 2018). The propositions of driving people away from the drive of accumulation of wealth while sustaining a basic living standard or boldly redistributing resources more equitable presupposes the existence of sufficient economic surplus and high levels of human development. And it is not hard to see if and how these two conditions are satisfied in the Global South. The fundamental challenge for Global South instead is not only the existing inequalities in the distribution of this surplus but also the creation of sufficient surplus in the first place.

In a similar fashion, proposals of reducing working hours presuppose a high-wage economy with labor productivity. Such a condition would ensure that the access to basic living conditions would not be compromised by less working hours. An implicit assumption in such policies is the notion that full employment is already achieved, allowing thus workers to distribute their time collectively between them rather than embark on a vicious competition for employment or excess work time under the threat of unemployment. Yet as Kalecki (1984) notes, full employment is untenable under capitalist conditions exactly because it is necessary for their reproduction. Particularly if one considers the conditions of development economies the problem of unemployment or informal employment is even more accentuated (Chen & Li, 2021).

The implicit and explicit assumptions of post-growth and de-growth proposals may respond to the crisis of core aspects of the mainstream understanding of climate change. Nonetheless, they do not contribute to the critique of the systemic connections between capitalism and the climate crisis. They clearly fail to resonate with the realities of the Global

South and particularly those countries on the periphery of the global capitalist structure (Chen, 2023), and abstract from and isolate the environmental and development crisis of the developing countries in their analysis. Constraining the discussion in terms of political feasibility evades the inherent tendencies of capitalism deepening climate change and ousts radical proposals that transcend the capitalist mode of production. Deliberating these policies in a political economic vacuum while neglecting the complex challenges faced by Global South indicates a deeper failure to acknowledge the development challenges of the Global South and their interconnectedness of this triplet crisis.

5 Recognizing the Interconnectedness of the Triplet Crisis: Ecological Imperialism and Ecological Colonialism

So far, the frameworks presented here have failed in responding to the interconnectedness of the triplet crisis marked by the intensifying climate emergency, the inadequacy of mainstream economics to meaningfully engage with ecological breakdown, and the entangled environmental and developmental struggles facing the Global South. The overlap between the environmental predicament and the crisis in the Economics' understanding of climate change necessitate alternative frameworks that firmly restate the socio-economic basis and particularly the role of capitalism in the climate catastrophe. Simultaneously, these alternative perspectives should weigh in the complex challenges forming the environmental and development crisis of the Global South. Towards that direction, radical frameworks both within and outside political economics constitute a promising initial step.

Ecological Imperialism and Ecological colonialism are two concepts that recognize the crisis of climate and the failure of mainstream economics while resituating the connection between Global South, affected communities, and modalities of colonization and exploitation. Ecological imperialism stems from the tradition of Marxist political economy while ecological colonialism is mostly employed by post-colonial and post-development scholars. However, ecological colonialism, unlike ecological imperialism, lacks terminological coherence, due to the nuanced distinctions among and often interchangeable use of interrelated concepts and terms (García López & Navas, 2019). To understand how these two concepts challenge the "canonical" ways of reasoning we must first distinguish between them. The Marxist approach seeks to underpin the economic, political, and ideological *processes* essential to capitalist accumulation that bring about and reinforce ecological imperialism while the post-colonial and post-development perspectives emphasize predominately the *impacts* of ecological colonialism on the relation between natural environment and affected communities.

Aspects of ecological imperialism were recognized early on in the political economy of Kwame Nkrumah (1966) and Walter Rodney (1981). These authors recognized an essential feature of the imperialist practice where the appropriation of natural resources of peripheral economies by the core left a "scramble" for the former, reinforcing their underdevelopment to the benefit of Western powers. These authors forcefully showed how such processes are not accidental phenomena but embedded in the colonial legacies that persist under neo-colonialism. In retrospect, the dominance of extractivism, land-grabbing acts and structural adjustment programs that transform the periphery into a profitable but socially and environmentally devastated ground demonstrate the endurance of colonial legacies and contemporary modalities as essential features of ecological imperialism (Frame, 2016).

In the more contemporary literature, Foster and Clark (2004) offer one of the most influential analyses of "ecological imperialism". In their analysis, they highlight the inherent ecological contradictions of capitalism and relate ecological imperialism to two key aspects. The first aspect of the irreparable *metabolic rift*, created by capitalist relations and the endless drive for capital accumulation, refers to the ongoing disruption of Earth's natural metabolism by the social metabolic order of capital, exacerbating ecological contradictions (see Foster et al., 2010; Foster, 1999). The second aspect of unequal ecological exchange, in turn, addresses the unequal exchanges of material ecological flows between developed and developing countries (Clark & Foster, 2009; Foster & Holleman, 2014). Among the key aspects of ecological imperialism are the appropriation and transformation of ecosystems, the dominance of extractive industries, the exploitation of ecological vulnerabilities for strategic control, and the dumping of waste practices by the dominant capitalist nations (Foster & Clark, 2004). Ecological imperialism is found historically in examples such as the Guano-Nitrate trade, where millions of tons of guano and nitrates were sent from Peru and Chile to Great Britain and other Global North economies. This trade relied on heavily exploited Chinese laborers, who were imported specifically for the purpose of this trade, to counteract the declining fertility of impoverished rural lands (Clark & Foster, 2009). Notwithstanding, far from being just a phenomenon of the past, ecological imperialism is also found in more contemporary cases such as the oil curse, where reserves of oil located in poor countries make them a political and military target of dominant forces, and the ecological debt, driven by the socio-ecological devastation within nations under the umbrella of ecological imperialism and the appropriation of the global commons and the inequalities in the use of their absorption capacity. (Foster & Clark, 2004).

Further work on ecological imperialism, such as Frame (2016, 2022), contributes significantly in the contextualization of its core characteristics.[4] The very concept is intrinsically connected with the capitalist social relations and the economic mechanisms of capitalism that propel capitalist accumulation. The span of ecological imperialism is inherently global and is mediated by a world hierarchical system rooted in colonialism and reinforced by unequal economic, political, military, and ideological power while its socio-ecological impacts are disproportionately skewed against the peripheral countries while benefiting the capitalist core. The various concrete forms ecological imperialism takes across time and space are not predetermined but rather the outcome between social resistance and counter-resistance (Frame, 2016).

Ecological imperialism includes a set of economic, political as well as ideological mechanisms of dominance. For example, the Western climate consensus may appear ostensibly technocratic, developmentalist, and progressive, but is in its essence "highly political as a result of its ahistorical, North-centric, and capitalist-conformist approach" (Chen, 2022, p. 477). Such narratives over climate change shift the accountability from the Global North to the Global South and inherently reflect the unequal power dynamics between nations and work to perpetuate "the overarching system of ecological imperialism" to the detriment of the

[4] According to Frame (2016, 90) ecological imperialism can be defined as "the subjugation of the economic, political, and/or social institutions of a (generally peripheral) country for the biophysical, metabolic needs of the (generally core or semi-periphery), inextricable from the purpose of making such resources accessible and amenable (in the right quantities and for the right price) to the needs of (foreign) capital accumulation", and the study of imperialism as the process of "[u]nderstanding the structures and policies that ensure the continued flow of both resources and profit from certain regions and social groups to other regions and social groups".

Global South (Chen, 2022, p. 475). In this sense, Ecological imperialism operates through a broad range of economic, political, and ideological processes connected with the wider imperatives of capitalist accumulation.

On the other hand, post-development and post-colonial studies focus on the impacts of ecological colonialism rather than the systemic sources as in ecological imperialism. A seminal work in this field by environmental historian Alfred Crosby (1986) highlights the biological dimensions of ecological imperialism, documenting how invasive species, diseases and colonial land-use practices devastated natural biodiversity and decimated millions of native inhabitants.

Among the central themes in ecological colonialism are the post-development critiques of Western or Eurocentric ideology of development (Escobar, 2011) and the alliance between post-colonialism and ecocritical approaches (Huggan & Tiffin, 2015; Mount & O'Brien, 2013). According to Njoh (2022, p. 584), environmental colonialism examines how "colonialism has impacted nature, land, animals, and people in former colonies" while "post-colonial environmentalism" provides a "systematic and analytical interrogation of the environmental implications of the colonial project".

Acts of appropriation of land and resources from indigenous populations as well as the physical elimination of the communities themselves are indispensable aspects of colonialism (Bacon, 2018). Furthermore, as illustrated from different angles such as the critical analysis of post-colonial and Western literature, the dominance of colonial discourses of nature and environment over indigenous practices violently shifts the existing practices and relations of the communities with the natural world (people—animals—environment) and establishes ontological and epistemological attitudes that emphasize the dominance of humans over the natural environment (Huggan & Tiffin, 2015; Mount & O'Brien, 2013; Njoh, 2022; Whyte, 2018). As Bacon (2018, 3) and Domínguez and Luoma (2020) illustrate with examples from North America, Asia, and Africa, which include displacing indigenous population for the building of national parks, these patterns are still prevalent in mainstream environmental movements of wilderness, conservation, and preservation, which often sideline concerns of social justice and the Indigenous peoples as active actors. Lastly, political and discursive forms of elimination, exemplify what is often referred to as "ecological violence" (Bacon, 2018). This form of violence constitutes a defining characteristic of the disruption of eco-social relations that undermines the social resilience and collective continuance of Indigenous peoples, as Whyte (2018) illustrates with the example of US strategies against the Anishinaabe peoples inhabiting the Great Lakes region of North America.

Overall, these two concepts engage with aspects that are essential to understanding and responding to the triplet crisis—such as the connections between climate crisis, capitalist accumulation, and exploitation, global hierarchies, colonial legacies, neocolonial structures, and various forms of eco-social disruption and ecological violence against communities of the Global South. The Marxist tradition emphasizes the materialist foundations of capitalism and connects the climate crisis and the complex challenges of the Global South with capitalist accumulation driving the appropriation of nature within a hierarchical world capitalist system. On the other hand, ecological colonialism deepens the analysis of the impacts of climate crisis primarily by exploring its' immaterial dimensions in the sphere of ideological, representational, and imaginary on a "local" level. The analytical preference of post-development and post-colonial studies of ecological colonialism to imperialism is not arbitrary but rather connected with the use of colonization separated from the wider imperatives of capitalism as the primary category of analysis.

6 Conclusion

As this chapter argued, the majority of existing theoretical frameworks do not recognize the interconnectedness between the climate crisis, the failure of the Economics' discipline to analyze and respond to the climate emergency, and the complex environmental and developmental challenges of the Global South. The failure of mainstream economics exacerbated the severeness of climate change and led to a long period of policy inaction. Critics of the mainstream may bring clarity to the ecological limits and the dangers of growth but can neither firmly situate the role of capitalist imperatives in the climate crisis nor recognize the challenges faced by the Global South. The triplet crisis and the failure of these frameworks indicate that the challenges of the decolonization and decarbonization of Economics constitute a *unity*—they need to be pursued simultaneously as the only means to decisively respond to the contemporary ecological emergency.

From this perspective, the decarbonization and decolonization requires centering the interests and needs of the Global South. Instead of treating the Global South as a passive participant in the effort of decarbonization, it is most important to understand the global nature of the forms of ecological subordination and appropriation and recognize the laboring classes and communities of Global South as active parts of the effort of transcending the acute and capitalistically induced climate crisis. In this sense, the need to expose ecological imperialism and colonialism and their deleterious impacts on the Global South is more urgent than ever. Engaging with these concepts needs to come nonetheless with recognition of their analytical differences. On the whole, these frameworks are best qualified to resist the reproduction of the sources and systemic structures that induce a wide set of adverse socio-ecological impacts, a crucial step towards the eventual decarbonization and decolonization of the Economics discipline.

References

Almulhim, A. I., Alverio, G. N., Sharifi, A., et al. (2024). Climate-induced migration in the Global South: An in-depth analysis. *NPJ Climate Action*. https://doi.org/10.1038/s44168-024-00133-1

Arrow, K., Dasgupta, P., Goulder, L., Daily, G., Ehrlich, P., Heal, G., Levin, S., Mäler, K.-G., Schneider, S., Starrett, D., & Walker, B. (2004). Are we consuming too much? *Journal of Economic Perspectives, 18*(3), 147–172. https://doi.org/10.1257/0895330042162377

Bacon, J. M. (2018). Settler colonialism as eco-social structure and the production of colonial ecological violence. *Environmental Sociology, 5*(1), 59–69.

Binns, T. (2006). E. F. (Fritz) Schumacher. In D. Simon (Ed.), *Fifty key thinkers of development* (pp. 218–223). Routledge.

Chen, Y. (2022). How has ecological imperialism persisted? A Marxian critique of the Western climate consensus. *American Journal of Economics and Sociology, 81*(3), 473–501.

Chen, Y. (2023). Degrowth—What's in a name? Assessing degrowth's political implications. *Monthly Review, 75*(3), 1.

Chen, Y., & Li, A. (2021). Global green new deal: A global south perspective. *The Economic and Labour Relations Review, 32*(2), 170–189. https://doi.org/10.1177/10353046211015765

Clark, B., & Foster, J. B. (2009). Ecological imperialism and the global metabolic rift: Unequal exchange and the guano/nitrates trade. *International Journal of Comparative Sociology, 50*(3–4), 311–334.

Crosby, A. W. (1986). *Imperialism: The biological expansion of Europe, 900–1900*. Cambridge University Press.

Daly, H. E. (2015). Economics for a full world. *Great Transition Initiative, June*. Retrieved January 22, 2025, from https://greattransition.org/publication/economics-for-a-full-world

Daly, H. E., Czech, B., Trauger, D. L., Rees, W. E., Grover, M., Dobson, T., & Trombulak, S. C. (2007). Are we consuming too much—For what? *Conservation Biology, 21*(5), 1167–1169. https://doi.org/10.1111/j.1523-1739.2007.00770.x

Domínguez, L., & Luoma, C. (2020). Decolonizing conservation policy: How colonial land and conservation ideologies persist and perpetuate indigenous injustices at the expense of the environment. *Land, 9*(3), 65.

Escobar, A. (2011). *Encountering development*. Princeton University Press.

Foster, J. B. (1999). Marx's theory of metabolic rift: Classical foundations for environmental sociology. *American Journal of Sociology, 105*(2), 366–405. https://doi.org/10.1086/210315

Foster, J. B., & Clark, B. (2004). Ecological imperialism: The curse of capitalism. *Socialist Register, 40*, 186–201.

Foster, J. B., Clark, B., & York, R. (2010). *The ecological rift: Capitalism's war on the earth*. NYU Press.

Foster, J. B., & Holleman, H. (2014). The theory of unequal ecological exchange: A Marx–Odum dialectic. *The Journal of Peasant Studies, 41*(2), 199–233. https://doi.org/10.1080/03066150.2014.889687

Frame, M. L. (2016). The neoliberalization of (African) nature as the current phase of ecological imperialism. *Capitalism Nature Socialism, 27*(1), 87–105.

Frame, M. (2022). Ecological imperialism: A world-systems approach. *American Journal of Economics and Sociology, 81*(1), 503–534.

García López, G. A., & Navas, G. (2019). Eco-imperial relations: The roots of dispossessive and unequal accumulation. In I. Ness & Z. Cope (Eds.), *The Palgrave encyclopedia of imperialism and anti-imperialism*. Palgrave Macmillan.

Hänsel, M. C., Drupp, M. A., Johansson, D. J. A., Nesje, F., Azar, C., Freeman, M., Groom, B., & Sterner, T. (2020). Climate economics support for the UN climate targets. *Nature Climate Change, 10*, 781–789. https://doi.org/10.1038/s41558-020-0833-x

Hickel, J. (2018, December 6). The Nobel Prize for climate catastrophe. *Foreign Policy*. https://foreignpolicy.com/2018/12/06/the-nobel-prize-for-climate-catastrophe/

Hickel, J. (2020). What does degrowth mean? A few points of clarification. *Globalizations, 18*(7), 1105–1111.

Huggan, G., & Tiffin, H. (2015). *Postcolonial ecocriticism: Literature, animals, environment* (2nd ed.). Taylor & Francis Group.

Intergovernmental Panel on Climate Change (IPCC). (2014). *Climate change 2022: Impacts, adaptation and vulnerability*. Cambridge University Press. https://doi.org/10.1017/9781009325844

Jackson, T. (2021). *Post growth: Life after capitalism*. Polity Press.

Kalecki, M. (1984). Political aspects of full employment. In *The political economy: Readings in the politics and economics of American public policy* (pp. 27–31). Routledge (Original work published 1942).

Kallis, G. (2015, February). *The degrowth alternative*. Great Transition Initiative. https://base.socioeco.org/docs/paper-kallis.pdf

Kallis, G., Kostakis, V., Lange, S., Muraca, B., Paulson, S., & Schmelzer, M. (2018). Research on degrowth. *Annual Review of Environment and Resources, 43*, 291–316.

Keen, S. (2021). The appallingly bad neoclassical economics of climate change. *Globalizations, 18*(7), 1149–1177. https://doi.org/10.1080/14747731.2020.1807856

Likaj, X., Jacobs, M., & Fricke, T. (2022). Growth, degrowth or post-growth? Towards a synthetic understanding of the growth debate. *Basic Papers, 02/2022*. Forum for a New Economy. Retrieved January 22, 2025, from https://www.econstor.eu/handle/10419/281436

McRobie, G. (1974). Technology for development—"Small is beautiful." *Journal of the Royal Society of Arts, 122*(5212), 214–224.

McRobie, G. (1981). *Small is possible* (1st ed.). Harper & Row.

Morgan, J., & Daly, H. (2019). The importance of ecological economics: An interview with Herman Daly. *Real-World Economics Review, 90*, 137–154.

Mount, D., & O'Brien, S. (2013). Postcolonialism and the environment. In G. Huggan (Ed.), *The Oxford handbook of postcolonial studies*. Oxford Academic.

Njoh, A. J. (2022). French ecological imperialism: A postcolonial approach. *American Journal of Economics and Sociology, 81*, 581–619.

Nkrumah, K. (1966). *Neo-colonialism: The last stage of imperialism*. International Publishers.

Nordhaus, W. D. (1977). Strategies for the control of carbon dioxide. *Cowles Foundation Discussion Papers, 675*. Retrieved January 22, 2025, from https://elischolar.library.yale.edu/cowles-discussion-paper-series/675

Nordhaus, W. D. (1991). To slow or not to slow: The economics of the greenhouse effect. *The Economic Journal, 101*(407), 920–937. https://doi.org/10.2307/2233864

Paech, N. (2017). Post-growth economics. In C. L. Spash (Ed.), *Routledge handbook of ecological economics* (p. 10). Routledge.

Petschow, U., Lange, S., Hofmann, D., Pissarskoi, E., Aus Dem Moore, N., Korfhage, T., & Schoofs, A. (2020). Social well-being within planetary boundaries: The precautionary post-growth approach. *Texte, 234*, 1.

Quante, L., Willner, S. N., Otto, C., et al. (2024). Global economic impact of weather variability on the rich and the poor. *Nature Sustainability, 7*, 1419–1428. https://doi.org/10.1038/s41893-024-01430-7

Rodney, W. (1981). *How Europe underdeveloped Africa*. Howard University Press.

Rostow, W. W. (1960). *The stages of economic growth: A non-communist manifesto*. Cambridge University Press.

Royal Swedish Academy of Sciences. (2018). *Press release: The prize in economic sciences 2018*. Retrieved from https://www.nobelprize.org/prizes/economic-sciences/2018/press-release/

Schumacher, E. F. (1973). *Small is beautiful: Economics as if people mattered*. Harper & Row.

Singh, P. (2023). Celebrating the 50th anniversary of Schumacher's small is beautiful: An eco-socialist perspective. *Capitalism Nature Socialism, 34*(4), 1–19.

Toye, J. (2012). The world improvement plans of Fritz Schumacher. *Cambridge Journal of Economics, 36*(2), 387–403.

UNDP (United Nations Development Programme). (2024). Human development report 2023–24: Breaking the gridlock: Reimagining cooperation in a polarized world. New York.

Varian, H. R. (1992). *Microeconomic analysis* (3rd ed.). W. W. Norton & Company.

Varma, R. (2003). E.F. Schumacher: Changing the paradigm of bigger is better. *Bulletin of Science, Technology and Society, 23*, 114–124. https://doi.org/10.1177/0270467603251313

Weitzman, M. L. (2011). Revisiting fat-tailed uncertainty in the economics of climate change. *Review of Environmental Economics and Policy, 5*(2), 275–292.

Whyte, K. (2018). Settler colonialism, ecology, and environmental injustice. *Environment and Society, 9*(1), 125–144.

World Meteorological Organization (WMO). (2023). *Atlas of mortality and economic losses from weather, climate and water extremes (1970–2021)*. WMO-No. 1267. Geneva: WMO. Retrieved from https://library.wmo.int/doc_num.php?explnum_id=11178

World Meteorological Organization. (2025). WMO confirms 2024 as warmest year on record at about 1.55 °C above pre-industrial level. Retrieved from https://wmo.int/news/media-centre/wmo-confirms-2024-warmest-year-record-about-155degc-above-pre-industrial-level

Rethinking the Food System: Looking Within, Looking Ahead

Harshita Bhasin

Abstract The widespread recognition of the large ecological footprint of agriculture as well as its vulnerability to climate change has led to the emergence of competing visions of a sustainable and resilient food system. This chapter provides an overview of the current landscape of the global food system as well as new tendencies in the food and climate politics reshaping it. In doing so, it argues that mainstream discourse on agri-food system fails to recognize ecological degradation as an inherent tendency of the capitalist logic which underlies the system and advances technological fixes to rebuild a more sustainable agri-food system. In contrast, an alternative approach based on food sovereignty and agroecology centralizes a systemic understanding of ecosystems as well as questions of power and justice in the agri-food system. It aims to overhaul the globalized and homogenized agri-food system dominated by agribusinesses to rebuild local, decentralized, and diversified agri-systems which prioritize the agency and autonomy of food producers as well as consumers. However, there are several political and economic challenges which this alternative agrarian imaginary must confront in order to operationalize its vision of a just and sustainable agri-food system.

H. Bhasin (✉)
Institute for Human Development, New Delhi, India
e-mail: harshita.bhasin@gmail.com

A. Agunsoye and A. Arntsen (eds.), *Decarbonising and Decolonising Economics*, https://doi.org/10.1007/978-3-032-11972-8_4

Keywords Agriculture · Food systems · Food sovereignty · Agroecology

1 Introduction

In his classic 1997 text "The History of Development: From Western Origins to Global Faith" Gilbert Rist provides an insightful definition of "development":

> 'Development' consists of a set of practices, sometimes appearing to conflict with one another, which require – for the reproduction of society – *the general transformation and destruction of the natural environment* and of social relations. *Its aim is to increase the production of commodities (goods and services) geared*, by way of exchange, to effective demand. (Rist, 2014: 13; emphasis added)

A key revelation from Rist's formulation is his emphasis on the destruction of nature and social relations as well as the pursuit of abundance as integral to the process of development. The obsession with material abundance in the mainstream development paradigm[1] is unsurprising if one notes McMichael's (2009) assertion that the term development is nothing but an ideological expression of capitalist development. Capitalist development by its inherent nature is centred around the pursuit of abundance. The belief that the pursuit of abundance shall achieve welfare for all has legitimized the development project at the global scale over the last seven decades. However, the working of the development project since the latter half of the twentieth century has been accompanied by unsurmountable levels of environmental destruction that jeopardizes the continuity of the development project as it is (Foster & Clark, 2012; Hickel, 2019).

In the context of the larger climate crisis which confronts us, the case of the global agri-food system stands out wherein a relentless pursuit of abundance has produced grave consequences for planetary health. Campbell et al. (2017) identify agriculture as a key driver pushing the Earth

[1] Mainstream development paradigm refers to the dominant school of thought in economics which considers economic growth as the primary goal of development. Furthermore, it advocates the pursuit of free markets and laissez-faire policies to achieve economic growth and efficiency (Bakehouse, 1970).

system over planetary boundaries.[2] As per IPCC (2019), Agriculture, Forestry and Other Land Use activities accounted for around 13% of CO_2, 44% of methane (CH_4), and 81% of nitrous oxide (N_2O) emissionsfrom human activities globally during 2007–2016, representing 23% of total net anthropogenic emissionsof GHGs. However, if emissionsfrom pre- and post-production activities in global food system are accounted for, emissionsare estimated to be 21–37% total net anthropogenic GHG emissions(ibid.).

There are several alarming statistics which emerge from the IPCC (2019) report which draw attention to the contradictions which underlie the rapid expansion of foodproduction to feed the growing human population: About 25–30% of total food produced is lost or wasted. While two billion adults are classified as overweight or obese, about 800 million adults continue to be undernourished.

A warming planet has widespread consequences for global food security as heat related and extreme weather events undermine food and livestock productivity. Furthermore, volatility in agricultural production has repercussions for livelihoods of millions of rural poor.

The widespread recognition of the large ecological footprint of agriculture as well as its vulnerability to climate change has led to emergence of competing visions of a sustainable and resilient food system. As the climate emergency intensifies, we are at a critical juncture when economic and social relations which characterize the global agri-food system may undergo major changes (IPES-Food & ETC Group, 2021). On the one hand, we are confronted with a technocratic vision which advocates technology as a central tenet for driving sustainability in the agri-food system (Herrero et al., 2020). This vision does not challenge the capitalist logic which underpins the agri-food system and its exploitative and extractive tendencies. Furthermore, it does not question the dominance of agribusinesses and their control over global food supply chains; in fact, its focus on sustainable agri-tech provides a new frontier for agribusinesses to expand its influence on the global food system. On the other hand, there has been a rise of counter-hegemonic food movements and

[2] They examine agriculture's impact over nine planetary boundaries: land-system change, freshwater use, biogeochemical flows, biosphere integrity, climate change, ocean acidification, stratospheric ozone depletion, atmospheric aerosol loading, and introduction of novel entities and find that agriculture emerges as a major to significant contributor to all of them (ibid.).

alternative voices which call for a remaking of industrial agriculture and its uneven power structures as imperative to building a just and sustainable agri-food system (Wittman, 2009). This alternative vision aims to reassert the agency of smallholders in the food production system and prioritizes local food cultures and markets. Furthermore, it aims to decolonize the agri-food system by overhauling the historical inequalities based on race, gender and class which underpin it as well as prioritize indigenous communities' access to resources and role in decision-making within the sector. The ongoing tussle between the competing vision for global agriculture has widespread implications for how we grow, buy and consume our food in the future.

While a large-scale transformation of our food system is imperative to avert the climate crisis which confronts us, there is a need to examine the new directions which lie before us and their adequacy to build a just and sustainable food system. This chapter aims to provide an overview of the current landscape of the global food system as well as new tendencies in the food and climate politics which are reshaping it. It does so by laying out how introduction of the Green Revolution in the 1960s intensified use of resources and external inputs in agriculture. In doing so, it shows that a technocratic approach towards ensuring adequate food supply for global population along with deepening of capitalist relations within agriculture impaired a balanced relationship between agriculture and ecology as well as amplified the power and influence of big agribusinesses over global agri-food system. However, mainstream discourse on agri-food system fails to recognize ecological degradation as an inherent tendency of the capitalist logic which underpins the system and aims to advance technological fixes to rebuild a more sustainable agri-food system. In contrast, an alternative agrarian imaginary based on ideas of food sovereignty and agroecology aims to challenge the capitalist relations which underpin global agriculture to rebuild a system which centralizes a systemic understanding of ecosystems as well as questions of power and justice in the agri-food system. However, there are several political and economic challenges which this alternative agrarian imaginary must confront in order to operationalize its vision of the agri-food system.

The rest of the chapter is organized as follows: Sect. 2 reflects on the capitalist remaking of the global food system and the extractivist logic which underpins it, Sect. 3 reviews how contemporary mainstream thinking approaches the challenge of decarbonization, sustainability, and resilience of the food system. Section 4 highlights the inadequacy of the mainstream development paradigm in addressing the multiple crises which confront the food system and puts forth an alternative decolonized vision for global agriculture. Finally, Sect. 5 concludes.

2 Food System and Extractivism

When viewing the global food system in a longer perspective, it becomes clear that its history is closely intertwined with the trajectory of capitalism and colonialism. In this section, I provide a brief overview of how the coming of Green Revolution in the 1960s accelerated the environmental degradation that results from the global agri-food system.

In the second half of the twentieth century, as the newly independent countries of the Global South reeled under hunger and famines, the Green Revolution was born out of the productivity fetish of the mainstream development project as a peaceful technological revolution that would end hunger in the developing world (Patel, 2013). Green Revolution, in a narrow sense, was a package of High Yielding Varieties (HYV) of seeds which, used in conjunction with fertilizers and controlled irrigation, could dramatically expand agricultural yields in the Global South and end hunger (Cleaver, 1972). The United Nations Statistics Division's Environment Glossary defines Green Revolution as "increase in crop yields based on cultivation of ***high-response varieties*** of wheat, rice, maize and millet, and intensive use of fertilizers, pesticides, irrigation and machinery" (United Nations, 2024). It should be noted that at the heart of the Green Revolution lay the same assumption that underpins the development project in general: deprivation is a consequence of lack of supply; hence, abundance is necessary to end deprivation. In this context, it is interesting to note that rigorous investigations by Amartya Sen, Jean Dreze and Rolando V. Garcia during the 1970s and 1980s into famines in India, Biafra and Bangladesh reveal that historically, food crisis have not been a consequence of food shortages but societal breakdowns such as war, unemployment, repression, or gender inequality (Cullather, 2010).

It is often presented that there was no alternative to the Green Revolution given the dire status of food security in much of the developing world. In fact, Green Revolution was a political project in the sense of its ambition to propel productivity through a "technocratic" solution that bypasses the issue of agrarian reforms; in particular redistributive land reforms in the developing world. Prior to the Green Revolution, the issue of land reforms was central to agricultural development policy discourse as skewed distribution of land in rural areas was seen as impeding economic development and dynamism in agriculture (Janvry, 1981). Redistributive land reforms aimed to take land away from landed elites with very large operational holdings and distribute it to rural households with no land or very tiny holdings, as well as impose a ceiling on size of farm sizes (Byres, 2004). There were several justifications which were provided for land reform policies such as its potential to dismantle rural power structures and feudal or semi-feudal relations perpetrated by landed elites which impeded investments and productivity in agriculture, as well as alleviate rural poverty by securing livelihoods of landless and peasant households by provisioning access to land (ibid.). Feder (1976) propounded that the anti-reform bias of World Bank rooted in sanctity of property rights failed to recognize that the most direct way to help the rural poor is to undertake difficult land reforms which correct historical inequalities in distribution of land.[3]

> As almost every-one knows, the quickest and most direct way to help the rural poor is to do away with the blatant inequalities in the distribution of land, by expropriating without compensation the entire landed oligarchy practically at one stroke, turn over the land to the peasants under an entirely new and more just land tenure system and thereby prepare the way for rapid increases in output, productivity and income, and undertake all the steps necessary (eg, the nationalisation of the marketing system) so that the benefits accruing to the peasants will not be whittled away by the enemies of the reform and of the peasants. (Feder, 1976: 533)

However, on account of complex geopolitical and local political factors which characterized the Global South, the Green Revolution was embraced as a technological fix to fight hunger as against the process of social reform which would have dispropriated the landed ruling classes. It is interesting to note here that around the time the Green Revolution kicked off in the Global South during late 1960s and early 1970s, the Club of Rome came out with its "Limits to Growth" report. However, even while ecological concerns around the Green Revolution were present at the time, they were ignored on account of narratives around hunger and poverty. This technocratic path had far-reaching social as well as

[3] See Griffin et al. (2002) and Byres (2004) for a contemporary debate on relevance of redistributive land reforms for agricultural development in the Global South.

ecological consequences: one, it sidelined debates as well as policy actions on land reforms which could have reshaped rural power structures; and second, it intensified the resource use and ecological footprint of the global agri-food system. In this context, it is interesting to note Oasa's (2010: 17) insight:

> The intensified pace of these ecological processes has occurred alongside the more commonly discussed social consequences in the form of rural proletarianization and social differentiation in capitalist agriculture. Fundamental to the discussion of technology and its consequences is the organization of production and its social relations. To speak of one is also to speak of the other.

Oasa's assertion hints that ecological degradation, like deprivation and inequality, may have been an inherent tendency of capitalist production. This line of thinking has been developed by Patel and Moore (2017) who propound that tendencies towards ecological degradation are integral to the nature of capital itself.[4] Drawing on their work, one is able to identify a crucial mechanism through which capitalism exploits nature, as technology creates a false perception of enhanced productivity by assuming away hidden ecological costs of the production process. Patel and Moore view capitalism not as an economic system but as a way of organizing the relations between the humans and the rest of the nature, advancing an idea of capitalism as a world ecology, i.e. a system of relations between power, production, and reproduction work through the web of life. For them, capitalist accumulation thrives on appropriating nature as cheaply as possible in the form of cheap food, work, energy, and raw materials. They explain cheapness to be a set of strategies employed by capitalism to appropriate all kinds of work, human, or natural, with as little compensation as possible. The framework of world ecology transcends the Nature–Society binary and weaves together the processes of accumulation of capital with the production of nature in a dialectical unity (Moore, 2010, 2011). Similarly, Wittman (2009) outlines that a sustainable metabolic relationship between society and nature characterized agriculture prior to the advent of capitalism through the process

[4] They posit that the contemporary geographical epoch is better termed as Capitalocene over Anthropocene given that the capitalist system and not natural human tendencies explain the impact of human activity on the planet.

of recycling of nutrients. However, creation of labour markets, and commodification of land and nature broke down this system as agriculture shifted from a local, small-scale, and diversified reproductive system into a productivity-driven, market-oriented system and globalized system. In this sense, deepening of capitalist relations in agriculture impaired a balanced relationship between agriculture and ecology.

The Green Revolution is often seen as one of several agricultural revolutions that have preceded a successful wave of capitalist development by provisioning "cheap" food. According to Moore (2010, 2011), the success of the Green Revolution is not embodied in a package of HYV seeds and chemicals, but an appropriation of the best ecological spaces with good soil and water resources. Ultimately, the Green Revolution reshaped how food was grown in the Global South as new lands and food producers became heavily dependent on an intensive use of externally bought inputs and gave rise to the dominance of agribusinesses in the food system. HYV seeds created a false notion of productivity by externalizing the additional soil and water resources they extracted from nature. By the 1980s, the United Nations recognized that that the HYV seeds were, in fact, "high-responsive" rather than "high-yielding" seeds (Newman, 2007). Weis (2010) outlines that the use of standardized and simplified biochemical inputs in global agriculture has increased vulnerabilities towards new pests, weeds, fungi, and diseases leading to a treadmill of dependence on these inputs. This is exhibited in the race to develop ever new chemical fixes as pests and weeds inevitably develop resistance. Furthermore, rising use of marketbought seeds, fertilizers, and pesticides in Global South has been accompanied by a loss of local knowledge and practices as traditional knowledge gets replaced by intellectual property of agro-input transnational corporations (ibid). The seemingly capital-intensive nature of the project foreshadows that Green Revolution essentially involved appropriation of spaces where cost of land, water and labour was very low. Hence, the success of the Green Revolution was "made through plunder as much as through productivity" (Moore, 2010: 405).

In this context, it is interesting to note Shiva's (1991) scathing critique of the Green Revolution, highlighting how the techno-political strategy of the Green Revolution aimed to create abundance by pushing nature's limits. She argues that the idea of development with its obsession in creating material abundance takes the form of dominating nature to combat scarcity. In the case of the Green Revolution, the goals of development were rooted in the assumption that technology could substitute for nature and expand its limits; however, the failure of such a strategy stems from its paradoxical nature: while it is assumed that technology could replace nature, the very nature of the technology necessitates a more intensive use of natural resource base.

Besides the resource and input-intensive nature of global agriculture, the Green Revolution also led to the emergence of transnational agribusiness firms. Clapp (2023) highlights that multiple levels of concentration characterize the global food system, undermining its resilience in the face of shocks, where a small set of countries have come to specialize in a select few stable grains which dominate the food system while a small number of firms and financial actors dominate global grain trade and input markets. As a result, food-importing countries depend on a highly volatile global grain trade for their food security.

3 A Technocratic Reimagining of Food System

The previous section unpacked the innate contradictions which characterize the relationship between capitalism, agriculture, and nature. However, the global scale of the ecological crisis which confronts us does not present a roadblock to the capitalist economic system. In fact, a large share of green proposals which confront us are pro-capitalist, aimed at furthering capitalist accumulation through commodification of nature (Selwyn, 2021).

Mainstream economics thinking does not view the climate crisis as an inbuilt tendency of capitalism, but as an external threat that confronts the system, a mere externality that may be corrected by introducing new technologies and expanding the logic of markets to the realm of nature. For instance, if the Green Revolution-induced intensive use of fertilizers and pesticides, then climate smart technologies can help farmers use precise quantities based on their soil health and farm conditions. If crops and livestock become continually susceptible to new diseases, then corporations must innovate and genetically engineer crops and livestock to wade off outbreaks. If industrial farming has accelerated biodiversity loss and carbon emissions of the agricultural sector, then expand markets for carbon and ecosystem payment services for preservation of biodiversity. However, these technological fixes do not question the dependence of agri-food system of external inputs such as synthetic fertilizers and pesticides or the diminished genetic diversity of crops and livestock which enhances their susceptibility to diseases or incompatibility of industrial farming geared towards monocrops and plantations with maintaining biodiversity. The World Economic Forum (2024), for instance, lays down the imperative for innovation to transform the food system and provides a snapshot of a futuristic vision which awaits global agriculture: climate smart technologies making use of satellite imagery and weather intelligence for precision agriculture, protein innovations and smart livestock monitoring, agricultural fin-tech, smart machinery using Artificial intelligence (AI) and robotics etc.

IPES-Food & ETC Group (2021) further outlines the technocratic vision envisioned by agribusinesses and food giants wherein precision technologies govern food production and personalized diets and nudging[5] change the world of food consumption. They predict an arrival of bio-digital food giants which use the urgency of climate crisis to advance technical solutions which allows them ever greater control over our food system. These include expansion of bio-engineering of crops and livestock as well as use of drones, AI and 'smart' machinery to automate farm-level decision making and farming operations to ensure precise quantities of inputs (seeds, pesticides etc.) are used; thereby, reducing farmers to mere 'digital outgrowers'.[6] The expansion of similar digital technologies and data-driven approaches in the realm of food consumption are likely to further homogenize diets and erode diverse food cultures as consumers surrender their food agency for personalized and optimized diets.

While the Green Revolution made food producers heavily dependent on big agribusinesses for agricultural inputs and homogenized diets of consumers by diminishing crop diversity, penetration of digital technologies allows agribusinesses to further deepen their control over all parts of the food supply chain from farm to table.

[5] The report uses the idea of "hyper-nudging" to refer to the combination of big data and behavioral science which may allow food industry to use the high volume of data harvested at the end of food consumers to continually track, micro-target and invisibly nudge their eating habits (ibid.).

[6] See Stone (2022) for a detailed analysis of how digital technologies in agriculture undermine farmers' decision making and autonomy. He theorizes the idea of "surveillance agriculture" in line with the larger tendency towards surveillance under capitalism with emergence of new information economies.

The corporate-driven, technocratic narratives towards the food system centralize the goals of allocative and distributive efficiency (through technological fixes) over inequalities and injustice which underpins the causes as well as impacts of climate change (Borras et al., 2022). Such an approach sidelines any debate on addressing the historical and colonial legacies of an unequal ecological exchange between the Global South and Global North. Unequal ecological exchange allowed a small set of rich countries to have a larger ecological footprint with little environmental degradation within their borders by importing resources (energy and materials) as well as externalizing environmental costs to the periphery.[7] Furthermore, external technocratic interventions imposed on the food producers in the Global South subordinate their local perspectives as well as indigenous knowledge of nature and ecosystems—thereby undermining their agency to reassert control over the corporatized agri-food system.

Proponents of the mainstream vision put forth technology as a win–win solution that can solve the intersecting challenges of decarbonization, climate resilience, and malnutrition without compromising on the goals of economic growth. They do not interrogate the productivist and extractivist tendencies (outlined in Sect. 2) which underpin capitalism. Selwyn (2021) underscores further that pro-capitalist conceptions of green transformations obscure how capitalism is based upon endless commodification of nature. This makes the adequacy of such approaches in resolving issues of decarbonization and climate change seem suspect as they are likely to deepen the capitalist relations which underpin climate breakdown. In fact, critiques argue that they may lead to large-scale land grabs, zoonotic diseases, antibiotic-resistant superbugs, increased volatility and supply chain disruptions as well as livelihood losses (Fairhead et al., 2012; IPES-Food & ETC Group, 2021).

Furthermore, these approaches fail to recognize the dichotomy between the Global North and the Global South: techno-fixes which work in the Global North may not be suitable for the agricultural landscape and agrarian livelihoods of the Global South. In fact, new pathways of green grabbing and green imperialism are likely to emerge through climate policies crafted without political economy considerations (Fairhead et al.,

[7] See Jorgenston (2006) and Foster and Holleman (2014) for a detailed discussion on unequal ecological exchange.

2012; Giles & Stead, 2022). More importantly, a technocratic reimagining of the food system is not an apolitical project, as several low-carbon policies advanced by mainstream thinking have implications for the rural world. Borras et al. (2022) propound that policies geared towards renewable energy drive extraction of resources from rural areas for biofuels, hydropower, solar and wind farms. Carbon-offsetting and sequestration schemes transform rural landscapes as global elites appropriate land and resources for environmental means such as carbon sinks, biofuel plantations, or biodiversity offset reserves so that local livelihood concerns are sidelined to pursue a global green agenda (Fairhead et al., 2012).

There is a need to interrogate the technocratic agrarian imaginary put forth by agribusinesses with questions of power and justice: should protein innovation[8] sidestep the question of unsustainable Western diets with their overconsumption of animal products? Can incentives for agroforestry to smallholders in the Global South, to offset carbon emissions in the Global North, eliminate the need to address questions of agency in climate action? What new forms of inequalities and loss of livelihoods emerge on account of large-scale automation of farm work? Should consumers empower AI and digital technologies to decide what they eat and how they buy food?

Approaches towards climate change which centralize questions of inequality and justice "identify a range of injustices related to knowledge (whose knowledge counts?), procedure (who is involved in deciding?), distribution (who gets which benefits and who suffers what costs/risks?), and correctives (how are past wrongs addressed?)." (Borras et al., 2022; 12).

Ultimately, the technocratic vision laid out by agribusinesses is inadequate to reimagine a sustainable and just agri-food system on two fronts: firstly, it does not recognize that ecological degradation of agri-food system is not exogenous to the system but an inherent tendency of the capitalist logic which underpins it; and second, it does not address the historical (between Global South and Global North) as well as new forms of inequalities (between agribusinesses and food producers as well as consumers) which govern the agri-food system.

[8] Examples of protein innovation include lab grown meats or meat mimics which are plant-based products that are genetically modified to mimic protein content of meat. Protein innovation is considered a high growth market for agribusinesses to manage the high carbon footprint associated with livestock rearing (IPES-Food & ETC Group, 2021).

4 Food Sovereignty and Agroecology: A Decolonial Vision

The rising power of agribusinesses in the food system has created transnational agrarian movements which aim to re-assert the agency of smallholders over their livelihoods. While these movements often find their origins in struggles against World Trade Organization (WTO) for fair agricultural trade, indigenous' rights, farmers' rights to seed etc., there have been increasing calls for an ambitious agenda of food sovereignty and agroecology from these movements. La Via Campesina, with its origins in 1993, is one of the largest agrarian and social movements with claims to represent over 200 million peasants, farmers and rural labourers from 182 organizations in 81 countries which is spearheading the agenda of food sovereignty at the global scale[9] (Borras, 2023). Food sovereignty is defined here "as the right of peoples to healthy and culturally appropriate food produced through ecologically sound and sustainable methods, and their right to define their own food and agriculture systems" (La Via Campesina, 2021: 2). The idea of food sovereignty represents a rights-based approach to transforming the food system, centralizing the agency and autonomy of food producers and consumers. This is in sharp contrast to the dominant agri-food system wherein smallholders and their livelihoods as well as consumers and their dietary choices are subordinated to the logic of markets and influence of agribusinesses and food giants.

With the heightened threat of climate-related risks[10] looming over agriculture as well as the unsustainable production practices of industrial agriculture, the idea of agroecology has been embraced by peasant movements along with food sovereignty:

> Agroecology is the integration of research, education, action and change that brings sustainability to all parts of the food system: ecological, economic, and social. It's transdisciplinary in that it values all forms of knowledge and experience in food system change. It's participatory in

[9] International Planning Committee for Food Sovereignty is the largest coalition of transnational agrarian and food movements which includes La Via Campesina as its member along with other movements (Nicholson & Borras, 2023).

[10] Increased temperatures, changing precipitation patterns and greater frequency of extreme weather events are expected to undermine food security via a direct impact on yields and an indirect impact on water availability and quality, pests and diseases as well as pollination services (IPCC, 2019).

> that it requires the involvement of all stakeholders from the farm to the table and everyone in between. And it is action-oriented because it confronts the economic and political power structures of the current industrial food system with alternative social structures and policy action. The approach is grounded in ecological thinking where a holistic, systems-level understanding of food system sustainability is required (Gliessman, 2016: 599).

A holistic and comprehensive understanding of ecosystems underscores the practice of agroecology as against mainstream understanding of ecological forces as sheer externalities to be accounted for. While industrial agriculture is characterized by large-scale farming of monocultures which are heavily dependent on an intensive use of chemical inputs, soil, and water resources; agroecology envisions small-scale complex farming systems adapted to local conditions with limited dependence on external inputs (Gliessman, 2018). Agroecological approaches emphasize the importance of indigenous and local knowledge and practices, envisaging diversified and integrated crop–livestock systems and direct market linkages between producers and consumers. In contrast to the centralization and concentration of an agribusiness-led technocratic agricultural imaginary, food sovereignty and agroecology prioritize local and decentralized markets and small value chains (Gliessman, 2018; Nicholls & Altieri, 2018).

Moreover, these approaches aim to overhaul the unequal power structures which characterize the global food system. This can ensure increased autonomy for food consumers and producers relative to large agribusinesses, as well as fairer agricultural trade between the Global North and the Global South. By centralizing notions of women and indigenous peoples, food sovereignty, and agroecology represent a decolonial vision for global food system. The Nyéléni Declaration that emerged from the Forum for Food Sovereignty, a gathering of 500 representatives from 80 countries in Mali in 2007, laid out the movement's struggle for:

> a world where….there is genuine and integral agrarian reform that guarantees peasants full rights to land, defends and recovers the territories of indigenous peoples,…assures decent jobs with fair remuneration and labour rights for all, and a future for young people in the countryside; where agrarian reform revitalises interdependence between producers and consumers, ensures community survival, social and economic justice, ecological sustainability, and respect for local autonomy and governance

> with equal rights for women and men... where agrarian reform guarantees rights to territory and self-determination for our people... (La Via Campesina, 2007)

Calvário and Desmarais (2023) documents how women's struggles for gender equality, led by rural and peasant women within the movement, have embedded feminism in the food sovereignty agenda. This is reflected in the movement's demand for women's equitable access and control over productive resources as well as its efforts to ensure women's representation and leadership in food politics and policymaking. In this context, it becomes interesting to note Tramel's (2020) assertion that as the rise of climate-related resource grabs reconfigures territories across forests, fisheries and farmlands, movements of agrarian, climate and social justice are converging and building alliances as an act of resistance.[11] She argues that class as well as identity politics have become central to these movements as they converge so that they address questions of redistribution as well as recognition.

Proponents of food sovereignty and agroecology posit that a systemic understanding of agroecosystems, along with emphasis on questions of power and equity, food sovereignty, and agroecology, may facilitate a sustainable and inclusive trajectory for the food system (Altieri et al., 2012; Gliessman, 2018; Rosset & Martínez-Torres, 2012). Niewolny (2021) underlines the need to address the challenge of dismantling the dominance of neoliberal-fuelled technocratic productivism in agricultural science and policy with an intersectional justice and human rights lens for a sustainable food systems praxis. This requires critical research and policy changes geared towards redistribution of resources and decision-making to communities most affected by historical inequalities of race-gender-class within the food system, as well as building safeguards for most vulnerable groups in the food system (ibid.).

[11] Tramel (2020) cites examples of recent social movements in Navajo Nation, Indonesia and West Africa which prioritised alliance building through convergence to resist against the surge of transnational enclosures based on climate change mitigation goals. For instance, in Indonesia wherein fishing communities livelihood is threatened by pollution on account of expansion of oil palm plantations, Indonesia Traditional Fisherfolks union (KNTI) is bringing together peasants as well as indigenous communities for a joint struggle for food sovereignty as well as climate justice.

However, there are several key challenges which underlie a large-scale adoption of food sovereignty and agroecology. The hegemony of mainstream economic thinking and its promise of growth continues to shape development policies. A futuristic vision of a food system with technology at the helm which avoids difficult questions of equity and justice may also find sway amongst sections of food producers and consumers. Furthermore, civil society has raised concerns of co-optation of the idea of large-scale food system transformation by multinational corporations and export-oriented countries in order to maintain colonial and corporate forms of control (Canfield et al., 2021).

5 Conclusion

"Ecological damage was long seen as a regrettable but necessary cost of growth, and as justifiable in terms of the benefits of "development". The two phenomena were treated as separate but reconcilable. This is no longer possible... The faith in "development" can no longer escape criticism, not only because it justifies huge increases in social inequality but because it has become dangerous, by compromising everybody's future." (Rist, 2014: xii–xiii).

The climate emergency presents us with a critical opportunity to reshape our economic and social system. It has also powered large-scale mobilizations across the world wherein social movements of race, gender, indigenous communities, labour and environment have converged and deliberate on possible decolonial visions of development. As crises of food, health and environment converge, demands for remaking our food system have strengthened. We find ourselves at a critical juncture when the looming threat of climate change may lead to relentless adoption of technology without much debate about its implications for equity (IPES-Food & ETC Group, 2021). While the futuristic visions put forth by agribusiness and multilateral organization seem to promise solutions to problems of climate change and poverty, there have been widespread concerns from alternative voices in the food system. They suspect that a transformation of food system based on techno-fixes will further consolidate power in the hands of agribusiness creating new and unexpected environmental dangers (Selwyn, 2021).

An alternative vision based on food sovereignty and agroecology recognizes the extractivist logic that is rooted in the productivity fetish of mainstream development economics and hence, conceptualizes ecological limits not as a technical constraint faced in our progress but as a political and social problem linked to our economic system. The food sovereignty approach calls for radical changes to the global agri-food system wherein the globalized and homogenized agri-food system dominated by agribusinesses is overhauled for local, decentralized and diversified agri-systems which prioritizes the agency and autonomy of food producers as well as consumers. This calls for civil society action towards directing research and development towards agroecological production practices, state support towards agroecology, integration of indigenous knowledge and participation within agricultural extension systems, creation of direct networks (short supply chains) between food producers and consumers which can help build sustainable and vibrant local food economies.

There are several political economy challenges to a sustainable and just transformation of our food system based on a decolonial vision of food sovereignty and agroecology: the inherent difficulty of scaling up, the power of transnational agribusinesses and rapid dissemination of techno-fixes, the role of state, the economic aspirations of rural populations in the Global South etc. In this light, it becomes instructive to reflect over Selwyn's (2021: 3) question "Is the end goal a better, greener capitalism, or a transcendence of capitalism, and what are the implications of the answers to these questions for political strategy?".

Ultimately, the rethinking of our agro-food system raises larger questions about our conception of development in economics. The urgent task before us is to reformulate our notions of development to adequately address the missing link of ecological limits as well as bring redistributive issues to the forefront of policy agenda. There is a need to enhance our understanding of nature and ecosystems in line with sciences as well as indigenous knowledge systems as our ideas of development undergo a dramatic shift in the face of rising global inequality and climate breakdown. This calls for a larger decolonization project towards theoretical knowledge systems in economics so that diverse perspectives and visions of development and sustainability emerging from the grassroots help us build alternative development imaginaries.

References

Altieri, M. A., Funes-Monzote, F. R., & Petersen, P. (2012). Agroecologically efficient agricultural systems for smallholder farmers: Contributions to food sovereignty. *Agronomy for Sustainable Development, 32*(1), 1–13.

Backhouse, R. E. (2005). The rise of free market economics: Economists and the role of the state since 1970. *History of Political Economy, 37*, 1.

Borras, S. M., Jr. (2023). La Via Campesina—Transforming agrarian and knowledge politics, and co-constructing a field: A laudatio. *The Journal of Peasant Studies, 50*(2), 691–724.

Borras, S. M., Jr., Scoones, I., Baviskar, A., Edelman, M., Peluso, N. L., & Wolford, W. (2022). Climate change and agrarian struggles: An invitation to contribute to a JPS Forum. *The Journal of Peasant Studies, 49*(1), 1–28.

Borras, S. M., Jr., Scoones, I., Baviskar, A., Edelman, M., & Selwyn, B. (2021). A green new deal for agriculture: For, within, or against capitalism? *The Journal of Peasant Studies, 48*(4), 778–806.

Byres, T. J. (2004). Introduction: Contextualizing and interrogating the GKI case for redistributive land reform. *Journal of Agrarian Change, 4*(1–2), 1–16.

Calvário, R., & Desmarais, A. A. (2023). The feminist dimensions of food sovereignty: Insights from La Via Campesina's politics. *The Journal of Peasant Studies, 50*(2), 640–664.

Campbell, B. M., Beare, D. J., Bennett, E. M., Hall-Spencer, J. M., Ingram, J. S. I., Jaramillo, F., Ortiz, R., Ramankutty, N., Sayer, J. A., & Shindell, D. (2017). Agriculture production as a major driver of the Earth system exceeding planetary boundaries. *Ecology and Society, 22*(4), 1.

Canfield, M., Anderson, M. D., & McMichael, P. (2021). UN food systems summit 2021: Dismantling democracy and resetting corporate control of food systems. *Frontiers in Sustainable Food Systems, 5*, Article 661552.

Clapp, J. (2023). Concentration and crises: Exploring the deep roots of vulnerability in the global industrial food system. *The Journal of Peasant Studies, 50*(1), 1–25.

Cleaver, H. M. (1972). The contradictions of the green revolution. *The American Economic Review, 62*(1/2), 177–186.

Cullather, N. (2010). *The hungry world: America's Cold War battle against poverty in Asia*. Harvard University Press.

De Janvry, A. (1981). The role of land reform in economic development: Policies and politics. *American Journal of Agricultural Economics, 63*(2), 384–392.

Fairhead, J., Leach, M., & Scoones, I. (2012). Green grabbing: A new appropriation of nature? *Journal of Peasant Studies, 39*(2), 237–261.

Feder, E. (1976). McNamara's little green revolution: World Bank scheme for self-liquidation of third world peasantry. *Economic and Political Weekly, 11*(14), 532–541. http://www.jstor.org/stable/4364513

Foster, J. B., & Clark, B. (2012). The planetary emergency. *Monthly Review, 64*(7), 1–25.

Foster, J. B., & Holleman, H. (2014). The theory of unequal ecological exchange: A Marx–Odum dialectic. *Journal of Peasant Studies, 41*(2), 199–233.

Giles, D. B., & Stead, V. (2022). Big data won't feed the world: Global agribusiness, digital imperialism, and the contested promises of a new Green Revolution. *Dialectical Anthropology, 46*(1), 37–53.

Gliessman, S. (2016). Transforming food systems with agroecology. *Agroecology and Sustainable Food Systems, 40*(3), 187–189.

Gliessman, S. (2018). Defining agroecology. *Agroecology and Sustainable Food Systems, 42*(6), 599–600.

Gliessman, S. R. (2020). Transforming food and agriculture systems with agroecology. *Agriculture and Human Values, 37*, 547–548.

Griffin, K., Khan, A. R., & Ickowitz, A. (2002). Poverty and the distribution of land. *Journal of Agrarian change, 2*(3), 279–330.

Herrero, M., Thornton, P. K., Mason-D'Croz, D., Palmer, J., Benton, T. G., Bodirsky, B. L., Bogard, J. R., et al. (2020). Innovation can accelerate the transition towards a sustainable food system. *Nature Food, 1*(5), 266–272.

Hickel, J. (2019). Is it possible to achieve a good life for all within planetary boundaries? *Third World Quarterly, 40*(1), 18–35.

IPCC. (2019). Summary for policymakers. In *Climate change and land: An IPCC special report on climate change, desertification, land degradation, sustainable land management, food security, and greenhouse gas fluxes in terrestrial ecosystems* [P.R. Shukla, J. Skea, E. Calvo Buendia, V. Masson-Delmotte, H.-O. Pörtner, D. C. Roberts, P. Zhai, R. Slade, S. Connors, R. van Diemen, M. Ferrat, E. Haughey, S. Luz, S. Neogi, M. Pathak, J. Petzold, J. Portugal Pereira, P. Vyas, E. Huntley, K. Kissick, M. Belkacemi, J. Malley, (Eds.)] (in press).

IPES-Food & ETC Group. (2021). *A long food movement: Transforming food systems by 2045.*

Jorgenson, A. K. (2006). Unequal ecological exchange and environmental degradation: A theoretical proposition and cross-national study of deforestation, 1990–2000. *Rural Sociology, 71*(4), 685–712.

La Via Campesina. (2007). *Nyéléni declaration: Forum for food sovereignty*, Mali. Available from: https://nyeleni.org/IMG/pdf/DeclNyeleni-en.pdf

La Via Campesina. (2021). *Food sovereignty, a manifesto for the future of our planet.*

McMichael, P. (2009). Feeding the world: Agriculture, development and ecology. *Socialist Register, 43*(43), 1.

Moore, J. W. (2010). The end of the road? Agricultural revolutions in the capitalist world-ecology, 1450–2010. *Journal of Agrarian Change, 10*(3), 389–413.

Moore, J. W. (2011). Ecology, capital, and the nature of our times: Accumulation & crisis in the capitalist world-ecology. *Journal of World-Systems Research, 17*(1), 107–146.

Newman, B. (2007). A bitter harvest: Farmer suicide and the unforeseen social, environmental and economic impacts of the Green Revolution in Punjab, India. *Development Report, 15*, 1.

Nicholls, C. I., & Altieri, M. A. (2018). Pathways for the amplification of agroecology. *Agroecology and Sustainable Food Systems, 42*(10), 1170–1193.

Nicholson, P., & Borras, S. M., Jr. (2023). It wasn't an intellectual construction: The founding of La Via Campesina, achievements and challenges—A conversation. *The Journal of Peasant Studies, 50*(2), 610–626.

Niewolny, K. L. (2021). Boundary politics and the social imaginary for sustainable food systems. *Agriculture and Human Values, 38*(3), 621–624.

Oasa, E. K. (2010). The political economy of international agricultural research: a review of the CGIAR's response to criticisms of the 'Green Revolution'. In *The green revolution revisited* (pp. 21–53). Routledge.

Patel, R. (2013). The long green revolution. *The Journal of Peasant Studies, 40*(1), 1–63.

Patel, R., & Moore, J. W. (2017). *A history of the world in seven cheap things: A guide to capitalism, nature, and the future of the planet*. University of California Press.

Perkins, J. H. (1990). The Rockefeller foundation and the green revolution, 1941–1956. *Agriculture and Human Values, 7*, 6–18.

Prizzon, A., Wiggins, S., Abdenur, A. E., Daggash, H. A., Dubash, N. K., Kimani, J., & Lopes, C. (2024). Climate and development: What opportunities, what threats? *Development Policy Review, 42*, Article e12810. https://doi.org/10.1111/dpr.12810

Rist, G. (2014). *The history of development: From western origins to global faith.* Zed Books Ltd.

Rosset, P. M., & Altieri, M. A. (2017). *Agroecology: Science and politics.* Fernwood Publishing and Practical Action Publishing.

Rosset, P. M., & Martínez-Torres, M. E. (2012). Rural social movements and agroecology: Context, theory, and process. *Ecology and Society, 17*(3), 1.

Shiva, V. (1991). *The violence of the green revolution: Third world agriculture, ecology and politics.* Zed Books.

Stone, G. D. (2022). Surveillance agriculture and peasant autonomy. *Journal of Agrarian Change, 22*(3), 608–631.

Tramel, S. (2020). Convergence as political strategy: Social justice movements, natural resources and climate change. In *Converging social justice issues and movements* (pp. 64–81). Routledge.

United Nations. (2024). *Environment glossary: United Nations statistical division.* UN Data. June 2. https://data.un.org/Glossary.aspx

Weis, T. (2010). The accelerating biophysical contradictions of industrial capitalist agriculture. *Journal of Agrarian Change, 10*(3), 315–341.

Wittman, H. (2009). Reworking the metabolic rift: La Vía Campesina, agrarian citizenship, and food sovereignty. *The Journal of Peasant Studies, 36*(4), 805–826.

World Economic Forum. (2024) *Mainstreaming food innovation: A roadmap for stakeholders.* Available from: https://www3.weforum.org/docs/WEF_Mainstreaming_Food_Innovation_2024.pdf

Navigating Mineral Intensity: Decolonising the Green Energy Transition

Yousef Ghorbani, Glen T. Nwaila, and Derek Hugh Rose

Abstract The transition to renewable energy is accelerating demand for critical minerals, making resource dependence central to decarbonisation efforts. This chapter examines mineral intensity in the green energy transition, analysing its sustainability, equity, and governance implications. It critiques how colonial extraction practices continue to shape global supply chains, reinforcing resource and economic disparities, particularly in the Global Majority (often referred to as the Global South). Decolonisation provides a framework for rethinking mineral governance, advocating for equitable resource distribution, responsible sourcing, and the integration of Indigenous knowledge systems. The chapter highlights the

Y. Ghorbani (✉)
School of Natural Sciences, University of Lincoln, Lincoln, UK
e-mail: YGhorbani@lincoln.ac.uk

G. T. Nwaila
The African Research Centre for Ore Systems Science (CORES), School of Geosciences, University of the Witwatersrand, Johannesburg, South Africa
e-mail: glen.nwaila@wits.ac.za

D. H. Rose
The African Research Centre for Ore Systems Science (CORES), University of the Witwatersrand, Johannesburg, South Africa

A. Agunsoye and A. Arntsen (eds.), *Decarbonising and Decolonising Economics*, https://doi.org/10.1007/978-3-032-11972-8_5

environmental and social costs of extraction and explores solutions such as circular economy models, supply chain transparency, and participatory governance. Empirical analysis reveals how contemporary mineral extraction replicates historical exploitation patterns, underscoring the urgency of policy interventions. Case studies illustrate how the alternative approach of community-led governance models foster sustainability by prioritising labour rights, environmental protections, and local agency. Achieving a just and sustainable energy transition requires moving beyond extractivist paradigms towards regenerative resource management. This chapter offers insights for policymakers, industry leaders, and researchers to reimagine mineral supply chains that balance technological advancement with ethical resource stewardship.

Keywords Decolonisation · Resource governance · Critical minerals · Sustainable and ethical mining · Circular economy · Green energy transition · Indigenous knowledge systems · Just energy transition · Supply chain transparency · Environmental and social justice

1 Introduction

The green energy transition marks a transformative shift in global energy systems, aiming to curb climate change and reduce greenhouse gas emissions. Renewable technologies such as solar panels, wind turbines, and energy storage are central to this transition, driven by the need to reduce fossil fuel reliance, which still accounted for 82% of global energy production in 2021 (BP, 2022). Despite international agreements like the Paris Agreement (UN, 2015), progress varies, demanding accelerated action to meet climate targets (IEA, 2023a, 2023b). A key challenge is the rising demand for Green Energy Minerals and Metals (GEMMs), essential for renewable technologies (Ghorbani et al., 2024a; Watari et al., 2019). Supply–demand imbalances, energy constraints, and geopolitical tensions complicate mineral access, reinforcing historical resource exploitation in the Global Majority and its socio-economic disparities (Michaux, 2021a, 2021b; USGS, 2024).

Energy density further complicates the transition. Fossil fuels provide high energy output per unit, forming the backbone of industrialised economies, whereas renewables require larger spatial footprints. This discrepancy challenges infrastructure adaptation. For example, in South Africa's Komati Power Station transition to solar, coal-fired generation infrastructure was decommissioned and replaced with solar PV systems and battery storage. While this supports decarbonisation goals, it delivers significantly lower energy output and required redesigning the transmission interface, land repurposing, and integration of grid-stabilising storage technologies (Nel & Marais, 2024; Tladi et al., 2024). A sustainable shift requires a combination of hybrid energy systems that integrate both renewable and conventional energy sources, along with advancements in energy storage technologies to manage variability and intermittency. Additionally, enhancing grid stability through smart grid infrastructure, flexible demand management, and decentralised energy systems is essential to ensure a reliable and resilient energy supply during the transition (Mao, 2025).

This chapter explores mineral intensity in renewables, examining its sustainability and governance implications. It highlights the need for equitable resource access, questioning governance models rooted in Western perspectives (Nwaila et al., 2024; Zhang et al., 2023). Localised mineral development can support socio-economic progress but must be aligned with environmental and human rights protections. Sustainable practices such as recycling, circular economy models, transparent supply chains, and community-led initiatives offer practical solutions. Achieving a just transition demands international cooperation, public–private partnerships, and decolonial policy frameworks. This chapter explores the resource nexus within the green energy transition, examining how mineral demand can be balanced with sustainability, equity, and justice. It addresses the material requirements of renewable technologies, the socio-environmental impacts of extraction, and the implications for Indigenous communities and human rights. Emphasis is placed on transparent and responsible supply chains, circular economy approaches, and inclusive governance. Drawing from interdisciplinary expertise in energy materials and chemistry, the chapter connects technical challenges in mineral processing and efficiency with broader issues of justice, access, and resilience. It offers policy-relevant insights into managing mineral intensity in a way that advances both decarbonisation and equitable resource governance.

The green energy transition is often seen as a necessary shift from fossil fuels to renewable sources, yet it has drawn criticism for reinforcing capitalist power structures under the guise of sustainability. Critics argue that it risks replicating exploitative resource extraction systems, particularly in mineral-rich regions, without addressing global inequalities (Villegas & Scheyder, 2023). This calls for scrutiny of who truly benefits from the transition. Investments in renewable technologies such as solar panels, wind turbines, and energy storage systems are widely regarded as essential for reducing emissions and addressing climate change (IRENA, 2024). However, concerns remain regarding their equity, accessibility, and adequacy, particularly within the Global Majority, where financial and technological constraints persist (IEA, 2023b). Without more inclusive strategies, the benefits of decarbonisation may remain unevenly distributed.

Simultaneously, the energy transition relies heavily on critical minerals including lithium, cobalt, and rare earth elements (USGS, 2024). The extraction of these resources often results in significant environmental and social consequences, including deforestation, water pollution, and the displacement of communities. Many mineral-rich regions continue to bear the structural legacies of colonialism, which shape current patterns of resource governance (Michaux, 2021a, 2021b; European Commission, 2023b). A decolonial framework challenges these Western-centric models and emphasises Indigenous sovereignty, local knowledge integration, and inclusive decision-making processes. For the transition to be just, renewable energy investments must align with principles of equity, justice, and inclusivity. While reducing fossil fuel reliance is essential, the growing demand for critical minerals intensifies socio-environmental pressures on already vulnerable communities (Nwaila et al., 2024; Zhang et al., 2023). A truly equitable solution would ensure that countries in the Global Majority can meet their energy needs without replicating colonial patterns of resource extraction and exploitation (Adarve Zuluaga et al., 2025).

Case studies highlight the urgency of this need. In Indonesia, nickel mining for lithium-ion batteries has led to environmental destruction and the displacement of Indigenous communities. In the Democratic Republic of Congo, cobalt mining for electric vehicle batteries is linked to child labour and hazardous working conditions. Across Latin America, lithium extraction has triggered water conflicts and protests over environmental degradation by Indigenous groups (Ciftci & Lemaire, 2023). While often celebrated as a solution to climate change, the green transition must be critically examined to avoid reinforcing global hierarchies. Without a decolonial approach and genuine engagement with those most affected, it risks deepening inequalities under the banner of sustainability.

A holistic, justice-centred, and participatory strategy is essential for a truly transformative and equitable energy future.

2 The Role of Minerals and Metals in Green Energy Technologies

The green energy transition relies heavily on critical minerals and metals to support renewable energy technologies and decarbonisation goals. However, this dependency introduces significant environmental, social, and economic challenges (Bickel & Mia, 2023). This section explores the concept of mineral intensity, the extraction and processing of key resources, strategies for sustainable resource management, and the need for decolonial approaches to ensure an equitable and just transition. Mineral intensity refers to the quantity of minerals and metals required to produce and sustain green energy technologies. This concept is fundamental to understanding the complex relationship between resource demand and sustainability in the energy transition.

As the global shift towards renewables accelerates, the demand for critical minerals, including lithium, cobalt, nickel, copper, graphite, manganese, and REEs has increased significantly (Michaux, 2021a; Sokolova et al., 2025). These materials form the backbone of essential technologies such as solar panels, wind turbines, and EV batteries (Jannesar Niri et al., 2024). For example, lithium-ion batteries rely heavily on lithium, cobalt, and nickel; REEs are essential for wind turbine magnets and EV motors; copper is vital for electrical wiring and infrastructure; and graphite and manganese serve crucial roles in battery anodes and cathodes (Mathieu & Mattea, 2021). However, while these minerals are essential for decarbonisation, their extraction and processing often reproduce the same extractive economic models that the green transition is supposed to replace. Critics, including those featured elsewhere in this volume, argue that branding the transition as 'green' can obscure its resource intensity and the associated risks of environmental degradation and social injustice.

To address these contradictions, a more inclusive and sustainable governance framework is needed. This involves moving beyond profit-driven approaches towards models that centre environmental and social justice, particularly in mineral-rich regions of the Global Majority. Key strategies include the adoption of circular economy principles, responsible sourcing, local beneficiation, and policies that reflect decolonial and participatory values (Ghorbani et al., 2024a, 2024b; Sokolova et al., 2025). Only by embedding these values into mineral governance can the energy transition become genuinely sustainable and equitable. Yet the urgency of such reforms is underscored by the mounting real-world impacts of extraction already being felt in mineral-rich regions.

The extraction and processing of critical minerals impose significant environmental and social costs. For instance, lithium extraction via brine evaporation consumes vast amounts of freshwater and disrupts delicate ecosystems, particularly in the arid regions of South America where water scarcity is already a pressing concern (Woodward et al., 2020). Meanwhile, REE extraction underscores global supply chain vulnerabilities, as its production is geographically concentrated, particularly in China, creating dependencies that pose strategic and geopolitical risks. The refining processes often involve hazardous chemicals, leading to soil and water contamination. The environmental footprint of these operations extends beyond immediate extraction sites, affecting downstream ecosystems and communities reliant on local water and land resources. The social consequences of mineral extraction are equally profound. Many mining regions, particularly in the Global Majority, face exploitative labour practices, poor health and safety standards, and limited local benefit from resource wealth (Carr-Wilson et al., 2024).

Communities in resource-rich regions, particularly Indigenous populations, disproportionately suffer from land dispossession, pollution, and loss of traditional livelihoods. Mining-related displacement and inadequate compensation further entrench socio-economic disparities, exacerbating historical injustices. While some reforms such as corporate social responsibility initiatives, voluntary sustainability standards, or limited compensation schemes have aimed to improve practices, they often fall short in addressing the structural roots of injustice. Truly addressing these challenges requires more than such incremental measures. Strengthening regulatory frameworks, enforcing labour and environmental protections, and fostering community-led resource governance are essential steps towards sustainable extraction practices (Dou et al., 2023). Innovations in mineral processing, such as low-impact refining techniques and increased adoption of recycling and circular economy models, offer potential pathways to reduce dependence on primary extraction while mitigating its most harmful effects. Without these measures, the push for critical minerals risks deepening the very inequalities and environmental crises that the green energy transition seeks to resolve.

According to the International Energy Agency (IEA), achieving net-zero emissions by 2050 will require a sixfold increase in mineral consumption, with EVs and energy storage technologies accounting for substantial portions of this demand (IEA, 2023a, 2023b, 2023c). Figure 1 illustrates the projected global demand for critical raw materials across key technologies from 2023 to 2050, highlighting the shifting dynamics of resource consumption driven by the green energy transition (IEA, 2024). The series of stacked bar charts provide a comparative outlook on six essential materials which are integral to renewable energy technologies. EVs and grid battery storage emerge as dominant drivers of demand across all materials, reinforcing the critical role of battery technology in decarbonisation strategies. The projected expansion of wind and solar photovoltaics further amplifies the requirement for REEs and copper, while the growth of hydrogen technologies and low-emission power generation also contributes to the demand for selected materials. The graphs illustrate a pronounced and sustained increase in mineral consumption over time, underscoring the long-term implications for resource security, supply chain resilience, and environmental sustainability.

Critics warn that unbridled expansion of the mineral industry risks exacerbating environmental and social harm. These projections highlight the necessity for strategic interventions, including enhanced recycling efforts such as the recovery of lithium, cobalt, and nickel from spent batteries, and the development of circular economy models, like product design for disassembly and extended producer responsibility (EPR) schemes that keep materials in use for longer (Valizadeh et al., 2024). EPR schemes place responsibility on manufacturers to manage the entire lifecycle of their products, incentivising design improvements, and ensuring end-of-life collection and recycling. Additionally, investment in alternative materials, for example, using sodium-ion batteries instead of lithium-ion, or iron and manganese-based chemistries in place of cobalt, can help reduce dependence on high-risk critical minerals. Without proactive governance, the surge in demand for these minerals may exacerbate geopolitical tensions and environmental pressures, ultimately challenging the very sustainability objectives that green technologies are intended to support (Jannesar et al., 2024).

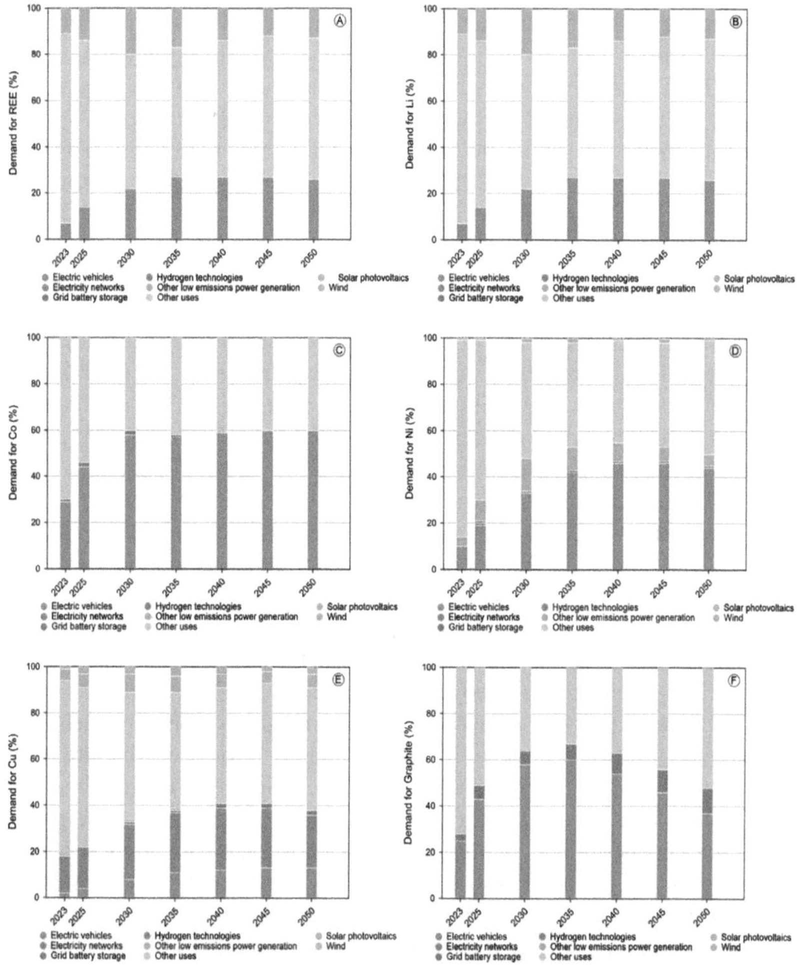

Fig. 1 Projected global demand for critical raw materials across key technologies (2023–2050) (IEA, 2024)

2.1 Decolonial Approaches to Mineral Intensity and Resource Governance

A just and sustainable transition requires more than technical solutions, it demands a decolonial approach, which places social equity, environmental care, and cultural respect at the heart of decision-making. This means rethinking who controls natural resources, how decisions are made, and whose voices are heard. Decolonial perspectives challenge dominant models of resource management that have historically been shaped by Western governments and corporations, often prioritising economic gain over community well-being and environmental health (Overland et al., 2022). One of the clearest examples of this imbalance can be seen in the mineral intensity of green technologies. The extraction of critical minerals in the Global Majority often reinforces historical patterns of colonial exploitation. Environmentally, mining contributes to deforestation, habitat loss, water pollution, and greenhouse gas emissions. Socially, it frequently results in the displacement of Indigenous populations, degradation of ancestral lands, and exposure to unsafe labour conditions and hazardous substances, often without meaningful consultation or compensation. These outcomes highlight the need for governance frameworks that prioritise environmental sustainability, human rights, and equitable benefit-sharing. A decolonial approach advocates for the restructuring of governance systems to recognise Indigenous sovereignty, promote fair distribution of resource benefits, and integrate local and Indigenous knowledge, developed through generations of sustainable land stewardship.

Importantly, the dominant frameworks that guide resource governance are shaped by Western-centric knowledge systems. These typically prioritise economic efficiency, technological innovation, and market-led growth, often sidelining environmental stewardship, community agency, and long-term equity. In contrast, Table 1 outlines principles from decolonial approaches, which aim to rebalance this dynamic by valuing knowledge systems and governance structures rooted in local contexts. Decolonial critiques also challenge the over-reliance on technical fixes, such as large-scale recycling, which, despite being part of Western policy responses, can offer only partial solutions if they do not address underlying structural inequalities or include community participation (Townsend & Roth, 2023). For example, while recycling is necessary for resource efficiency, its design and control often exclude producer-country communities, replicating existing power asymmetries. As global demand grows and mineral sourcing remains concentrated, geopolitical risks such as supply disruptions, price shocks, and political leverage intensify (Berthet et al., 2024). A decolonial lens calls not just for diversified sourcing, but for reframing governance to prioritise justice, equity, and inclusivity, particularly for communities in the Global Majority.

Decolonial perspectives highlight that the transition to green energy, while essential, must be fundamentally reimagined to avoid reproducing extractive dynamics. Mineral intensity should not be accepted as an

Table 1 Decolonial governance and knowledge integration

Key approach	*Description*	*Implications*
Integrating diverse knowledge systems	Incorporating traditional ecological knowledge (TEK); place-based knowledge developed over generations by Indigenous communities into resource management enhances sustainability and land restoration. Indigenous practices offer valuable insights into maintaining ecological balance while promoting responsible extraction	Stronger integration can improve resource resilience, but challenges exist in bridging Indigenous and scientific knowledge systems
Promoting Decolonial Resource Governance	Shifting decision-making power to Indigenous and local communities ensures inclusive governance. This involves participatory frameworks that empower historically marginalised groups	Strengthening local governance fosters fairness but overcoming entrenched power structures remains a challenge
Reforming Policy Frameworks	Transformative policies addressing structural inequalities can embed social justice and fair benefit-sharing in resource governance. Strengthening land rights and co-creating policies with affected communities ensures long-term equity	Inclusive policies enhance sustainability, but effective enforcement and political will are essential for lasting impact

Sourced from: Diver (2017), Youdelis et al. (2021), Gordon et al. (2023), Townsend and Roth (2023) and See et al. (2024)

inevitable cost of decarbonisation but rather approached as a challenge that requires equitable and innovative solutions. These include the expansion of recycling technologies, the integration of community-led practices, and a shift towards regenerative resource governance models. Short-term growth-driven approaches risk deepening existing global inequalities and undermining ecological resilience. In recent studies authors have underscored the importance of rethinking resource flows, governance structures, and power dynamics to ensure a just transition (Ghorbani et al., 2024a, 2024b).

A holistic and decolonial perspective therefore advocates for governance models that distribute benefits more fairly, protect ecosystems, and centre the rights and agency of affected communities. Inclusive governance, supported by investment in innovation and coordinated efforts across sectors can create new pathways for ethical supply chains, community empowerment, and regenerative resource practices. As Sakapaji et al. (2024) argue, such integrated models offer a route to a more responsible and sustainable future. Ultimately, realising this vision requires not only structural reform but also a transformation in how resources are valued, accessed, and managed (IEA, 2024).

Over-reliance on underdeveloped recycling technologies risks reinforcing extractive models. A just energy transition requires systemic change in resource governance, centring equity, justice, and environmental stewardship. Addressing mineral intensity demands efficient resource use, expanded recycling, and integration of Indigenous and community-led knowledge systems to ensure sustainability and inclusivity. The long-term success of the green energy transition hinges on its ability to balance economic growth with social and environmental responsibility (Ghorbani et al., 2024a, 2024b). An approach that prioritises short-term gains over lasting sustainability risks entrenching existing inequalities and undermining ecological stability. A more holistic and decolonial perspective challenges traditional models of resource extraction, advocating for governance structures that distribute benefits more equitably and mitigate the social and environmental costs borne by vulnerable communities. Navigating the complexities of mineral intensity requires more than technological advancements; it demands systemic change in how resources are valued, accessed, and managed. A transition that genuinely embodies sustainability and fairness must place community empowerment, ethical supply chains, and regenerative resource practices at its core. Only by addressing these structural issues can the green energy transition fulfil its promise of a just and sustainable future (IEA, 2024).

3 Challenges and Trade-Offs in Achieving Sustainable Mineral Supply

The green energy transition, associated with decarbonisation, has driven a surge in demand for critical minerals, creating a supply–demand imbalance that fuels price volatility. For example, lithium carbonate prices quadrupled within a year due to shortages, destabilising markets, and slowing renewable technology deployment (Jannesar Niri et al., 2024). Such fluctuations complicate economic planning and impact industries reliant on these minerals. Geopolitical tensions further exacerbate supply risks. Resource concentration in key nations, such as Chile, the home to the world's largest lithium reserves, raises the threat of trade disputes, regulatory shifts, and political instability affecting global supply chains (Ghorbani et al., 2024a, 2024b; IEA, 2023c). This calls for diversified supply strategies and fairer distribution of extraction benefits between producing and consuming countries. Despite economic theories suggesting mutual benefits through comparative advantage, in practice, we often observe a continued extraction of wealth from resource-rich producing countries to consuming nations, manifested through unequal trade terms, limited value addition locally, and weak regulatory frameworks. Figure 2 illustrates key factors driving supply chain instability, including supply–demand imbalances, geopolitical risks, environmental constraints, and systemic inefficiencies. Limited resource availability, trade restrictions, and carbon-intensive extraction processes heighten vulnerabilities, underscoring the need for sustainable resource management, recycling, and international cooperation to ensure long-term supply security.

This assertion of sovereignty disrupts traditional supply chain flows that have long favoured industrialised economies and multinational corporations, often at the expense of local development and environmental justice. Nationalisation and resource sovereignty have emerged as powerful tools for disrupting exploitative patterns of resource governance rooted in colonial histories. For example, Chile's ongoing policy debates about nationalising its lithium industry reflect a broader movement in Latin America to reclaim control over strategic resources and ensure that extraction benefits national economies rather than foreign interests (Overland et al., 2022).

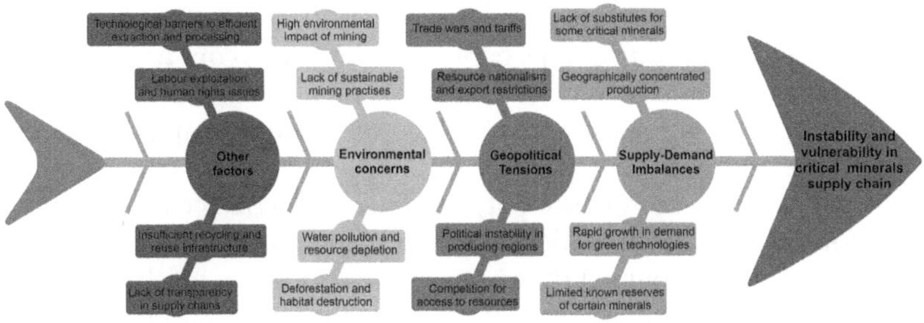

Fig. 2 Drivers of instability and vulnerability in the critical minerals supply chain

These discussions are not merely economic, they represent a deeper attempt to reconfigure power relations between the periphery and the core, prioritising long-term social and environmental outcomes over short-term foreign capital gains. Historical and recent events illustrate how resource geopolitics intersect with instability. During the Democratic Republic of Congo's political turmoil (2016–2018), cobalt production was severely disrupted, causing ripple effects across global battery manufacturing (Sovacool, 2019). Likewise, China's rare earth element embargo on Japan in 2010 exposed the fragility of concentrated supply chains and underscored how mineral-rich nations can exert strategic influence over technology-dependent economies (European Commission, 2023a). The emergence of resource nationalism can thus be seen not only as a geopolitical risk to consumers but also as a legitimate assertion of economic and political agency by producing nations, disrupting entrenched global inequalities. Reclaiming ownership, investing in domestic processing, and negotiating fairer trade terms enable producer nations to reshape mineral governance towards more equitable and sustainable outcomes. Moving forward, addressing the geopolitical challenges of critical mineral supply will require more than diversification and cooperation, it will demand a recognition of producer countries' rights to control their own resources, and a rebalancing of global supply chains away from extractive dependence.

While mineral extraction can stimulate economic growth and generate significant national revenue, it often exacerbates socio-economic inequalities in mining regions. Local communities, particularly Indigenous and rural populations, frequently experience land dispossession, environmental degradation, and a disproportionate share of the social and health costs, while receiving limited benefits (Palle, 2021). In Latin America, for example, Indigenous groups have voiced growing concerns about the adverse effects of mining on their ancestral lands, highlighting the urgent need for inclusive governance frameworks that prioritise human rights and cultural preservation (CSIS, 2021).

Achieving socio-economic equity in mineral governance requires more than formal regulation; it demands transparent benefit-sharing agreements, meaningful community participation, and policy mechanisms that empower local stakeholders to influence decisions that affect their livelihoods. A notable example can be seen in Australia's mining sector, where structured benefit-sharing models with Indigenous communities have been implemented with varying degrees of success. In particular, agreements such as the Indigenous Land Use Agreements and the Royalties for Regions programme offer valuable insights. These frameworks have enabled some communities to negotiate for royalty payments, employment opportunities, and social infrastructure investments (Singh, 2010). For example, in Western Australia, partnerships between mining companies and Aboriginal corporations have led to investments in housing, education, and health services, helping to redistribute some of the wealth generated from mineral extraction back into the communities affected by it.

However, the Australian experience also highlights challenges. In the South African context, the Royal Bafokeng and Bakgatla Ba Kgafela nations (viz. Manson & Mbenga, 2003; Mnwana, 2014) have agreements and ownership of mining corporations that exploit the platiniferous rocks on their ancestral lands to the benefit of the communities. The effectiveness of these agreements depends heavily on strong governance structures, legal enforcement, and community capacity to negotiate and manage benefits. In some cases, benefits have been poorly distributed or captured by local elites (i.e., South African traditional leaders), reinforcing internal inequalities. Nonetheless, these models demonstrate the potential for more equitable governance practices that balance economic development with social justice, particularly when local communities are treated as rights-holders rather than stakeholders. This underscores the importance of moving beyond extractive logics by embedding community agency and long-term development goals into mineral governance systems.

Embedding local knowledge and participatory approaches in mineral governance enhances sustainability and social inclusion. Indigenous communities possess traditional ecological knowledge (TEK) that informs land stewardship, biodiversity conservation, and long-term resource management (Gordon et al., 2023). These insights, refined over generations, offer alternatives to conventional extractive models that often prioritise economic returns over environmental and social well-being. In Canada, collaborations between Indigenous groups and mining companies have shown how integrating traditional land-use strategies can reduce environmental degradation while supporting culturally respectful economic development (Caron & Asselin, 2020). Strengthening participatory decision-making ensures that affected communities shape resource management policies. Inclusive governance structures foster equitable and sustainable outcomes by incorporating diverse perspectives (European Commission, 2023a).

Transparent consultation, community-led environmental monitoring, and co-management agreements are key tools for achieving this balance. However, entrenched power dynamics, restrictive legal frameworks, and corporate dominance often sideline local voices. Addressing these challenges requires institutional reforms that empower communities, ensuring governance frameworks integrate cultural and environmental considerations alongside technical expertise. A more inclusive governance model, built on transparency and respect for traditional knowledge, fosters resilience, reduces environmental harm, and aligns resource development with long-term social and ecological well-being.

4 Responsible Mineral Practices as a Pathway to a Decolonial Green Transition

The promotion of sustainable and responsible mineral practices is a cornerstone for achieving environmental sustainability, equitable resource management, and a just transition in the context of mineral intensity, decarbonisation, and decolonisation. This section examines strategies that not only mitigate environmental and social impacts but also critically reflect on the reliance on technological improvements and their implications for the global energy transition.

Resource efficiency is critical for minimising environmental impacts and optimising the use of scarce minerals in green energy technologies. However, the reliance on underdeveloped or non-existent technologies, such as solid-state batteries or sodium-ion alternatives, raises concerns about feasibility within the tight decarbonisation timeline (Yao et al.,

2025). While material substitution and advances in manufacturing, such as 3D printing, offer potential solutions, underinvestment in clean technologies by large financial powers poses a significant challenge. This underinvestment stems partly from fears of disrupting established industries and capital flows, highlighting the need for systemic change in funding and innovation ecosystems. A more critical reflection reveals that technological advances alone may not suffice to address the scale of mineral intensity challenges. Lifecycle assessments, which evaluate the environmental impact across the lifespan of renewable technologies, should guide design improvements. However, implementing these strategies at scale requires not only technological breakthroughs but also transformative policy frameworks and economic incentives.

Recycling and circular economy approaches are thus essential for addressing mineral scarcity and reducing environmental degradation. Strategies such as urban mining and product design for recycling offer promising pathways for recovering valuable minerals from end-of-life products (Spooren et al., 2020). However, the global recycling rate for critical minerals remains low, hindered by technological and economic barriers. For instance, recycling lithium-ion batteries faces challenges in material recovery efficiency and cost-effectiveness. To be truly sustainable and equitable, circular economy initiatives must critically engage with their dependence on global supply chains, systems that often concentrate economic benefits in the Global Minority while externalising environmental and social costs to the Global Majority. Addressing this imbalance requires rethinking where and how value is created and distributed within circular systems. This includes localising recycling infrastructure, investing in skills and technology transfer, and ensuring fair labour practices across the supply chain. Industrial symbiosis, where by-products from one industry serve as resources for another, can reduce waste and promote resource efficiency (Bender & Bilotta, 2020). Yet, these strategies must go beyond efficiency metrics and embed decolonial principles, placing local communities at the centre of decision-making.

Transparency and traceability mechanisms, such as blockchain technology and certification programs, aim to ensure ethical sourcing and compliance with international standards (Dou et al., 2023; OECD, 2021). However, these initiatives must be critically examined. As demonstrated in other sectors, regulatory frameworks alone do not guarantee adherence, labour rights violations and environmental abuses persist even under certified supply chains. Building trust and accountability requires ongoing stakeholder collaboration, independent audits, and meaningful engagement with local communities and Indigenous groups. Certification programs such as the Responsible Minerals Initiative (RMI) can offer a structure for responsible sourcing, but their effectiveness depends on whether they shift power dynamics or simply legitimise existing extractive models.

However, these systems are not without critique. Recycling processes can be energy-intensive and polluting, especially when involving complex materials like lithium-ion batteries and rare earth elements. The recycling industry frequently relocates waste processing and low-value recovery operations to the Global Majority, exposing vulnerable communities to health hazards and environmental degradation. This practice reinforces the very colonial hierarchies that decolonial frameworks seek to dismantle, transferring the environmental costs of consumption in the Global Minority to under-resourced regions in the Global Majority. Without addressing the systemic drivers of overconsumption and inequality, circular solutions risk becoming a green veneer that masks continued extractivism. Efforts to create a more ethical and equitable supply chain must therefore go beyond technological fixes. They must confront the structural imbalances in how resources are consumed, recycled, and disposed of, and who bears the costs. A decolonial approach demands that supply chain governance place environmental justice, Indigenous sovereignty, and community rights at the centre, not only during extraction but throughout the entire resource lifecycle.

Integrating TEK into mineral resource management presents an important opportunity to align sustainability efforts with cultural resilience. Indigenous practices offer deep-rooted insights into biodiversity conservation and land stewardship, which can inform more sustainable and context-sensitive mining practices (Diver, 2017). However, this approach must be undertaken with caution. Without proper attention to power asymmetries and historical injustices, the integration of TEK risks becoming a tokenistic gesture, used to legitimise extractive projects rather than challenge or transform them. Critics argue that TEK is often co-opted into technocratic or extractivist frameworks without truly shifting decision-making power or addressing colonial legacies. TEK must be central to decolonising resource governance, not treated as supplementary. This involves respecting Indigenous sovereignty, intellectual property, and community-led knowledge-sharing. Effective models from Canada and Australia show promise, but broader adoption requires strong legal frameworks, sustained investment, and genuine commitment to equitable power-sharing.

5 Collaborative Solutions for a Just Transition

A just transition in mineral resource governance necessitates collaborative, inclusive, and sustainable approaches that address mineral intensity, decarbonisation, and decolonisation. While international cooperation, public–private partnerships, Indigenous self-determination, knowledge co-creation, and decolonial policy frameworks are all integral to decolonial thinking (Bell, 2024), this chapter presents them as distinct yet interconnected pillars of a just transition. Each element contributes to reimagining governance systems that prioritise equity, transparency, and long-term sustainability. In particular, these approaches aim to move beyond extractive, top-down models by recognising the sovereignty, knowledge systems, and development priorities of resource-rich regions, especially within the Global Majority. Such frameworks offer pathways to align global energy demands with human rights, environmental stewardship, and social justice. International cooperation forms the backbone of sustainable mineral governance, providing a platform for inclusive and equitable frameworks that address the complexities of mineral supply chains (Russo et al., 2024). Key priorities include the establishment and enforcement of international standards to ensure responsible mineral extraction and trade.

However, the role of global institutions such as the United Nations and the World Bank must be critically assessed through a decolonial lens. While these organisations advocate for sustainable practices, they have faced criticism for perpetuating inequalities by favouring Global Minority interests (Berthet et al., 2024). It is important to consider the sovereignty of resource-rich nations and ensure that international agreements do not marginalise local voices. For instance, the geopolitical implications of lithium extraction in Chile highlight the tension between national interests and global supply chain demands. This section addresses these challenges, emphasising the importance of equitable resource distribution and the integration of local governance structures in international cooperation.

Public–private partnerships (PPPs) offer potential for aligning economic incentives with sustainability goals, but they are not without challenges. These partnerships have often been criticised for favouring corporate interests over local communities, thereby exacerbating existing power imbalances in the Global Majority (Sovacool et al., 2020; Sovacool et al., 2020, 2023). To ensure a just transition, PPPs must prioritise transparency, accountability, and inclusivity. Initiatives such as the Extractive Industries Transparency Initiative aim to enhance governance by disclosing financial flows and promoting community benefits. Promoting community benefits requires more than financial disclosure; it involves establishing mechanisms that guarantee equitable sharing of project gains, safeguarding local livelihoods, and embedding social investment strategies that are co-designed with affected communities (Wilson et al., 2021). Critically, PPPs must move beyond superficial engagement to foster genuine stakeholder collaboration, especially with Indigenous communities and local populations. Concrete examples of successful collaboration include frameworks where community benefit agreements and capacity building initiatives empower local actors to actively participate in decision-making processes (Smith et al., 2023). Such approaches strengthen local governance capacity, enhance trust, and ensure that community voices shape project outcomes. Addressing these shortcomings requires a deliberate effort to balance economic and environmental priorities with social equity, ensuring that PPPs genuinely contribute to sustainable mineral governance.

Achieving equity and sustainability in mineral resource governance depends on recognising and supporting Indigenous self-determination. The principle of Free, Prior, and Informed Consent ensures that Indigenous communities have the authority to participate in decisions affecting their lands and resources (Kusniati, 2024). Despite the significance of this principle, many regions lack robust legal frameworks to uphold these rights effectively (Reed et al., 2024). The absence of enforcement mechanisms often results in resource extraction projects proceeding without meaningful consultation, exacerbating historical injustices, and deepening socio-economic disparities. Many governments and corporations continue to prioritise economic efficiency over equitable distribution of benefits, often sidelining local communities in decision-making processes (Sakapaji et al., 2024; Townsend & Roth, 2023). Strengthening local governance structures and providing resources for capacity building are critical steps towards enabling Indigenous communities to assert their rights more effectively. Ensuring that these communities have access to financial, technical, and legal expertise enhances their ability to negotiate fair agreements and safeguard their interests. A governance framework that values

Indigenous knowledge and respects their sovereignty fosters resilience, supports long-term environmental sustainability, and reduces conflict between resource developers and local populations.

Sustainability efforts gain considerable strength when diverse perspectives are integrated through the co-creation of knowledge. Collaboration between academia, Indigenous groups, and industry fosters innovative solutions that align with local ecological and socio-economic contexts (O'Donnell et al., 2025). This interdisciplinary approach enhances understanding of resource governance challenges and helps develop strategies that balance economic development with environmental and cultural preservation. Educational programs that incorporate TEK alongside modern scientific methodologies play an important role in fostering mutual respect and collaboration. Addressing historical injustices in mineral resource management requires policy frameworks that prioritise cultural sensitivity, recognise Indigenous rights, and ensure equitable resource distribution. Decolonial approaches challenge traditional governance models by advocating for policies that respect local knowledge, strengthen community decision-making power, and shift control away from centralised authorities (Youdelis et al., 2021; See et al., 2024). When properly implemented, these frameworks contribute to sustainable resource management while safeguarding Indigenous sovereignty and cultural heritage. Policies that integrate TEK and local governance structures provide a foundation for long-term sustainability. However, reconciling global energy demands with decolonial principles remains a complex challenge.

Decentralised governance models empower communities by allowing them to control resource extraction within their territories, yet these models frequently face resistance from central governments and international investors who prioritise efficiency in supply chains (Ghorbani et al., 2024a, 2024b). The tension between economic imperatives and decolonial governance highlights the need for participatory policy-making processes that reflect the aspirations of all stakeholders. Examples from Bolivia illustrate how Indigenous-led resource governance can yield more equitable and sustainable outcomes. The country has established policies that grant Indigenous communities a formal role in mineral resource decision-making, demonstrating that inclusive governance structures can create alternative models for resource management (Loginova et al., 2025).

Through incorporating perspectives that challenge extractivism models and prioritise community-led development, policy frameworks can transition towards sustainability without repeating the exploitative patterns of the past (Hine et al., 2023). A just transition requires collaborative solutions that address the intersections between mineral intensity, decarbonisation, and decolonisation. Strengthening governance structures, fostering international cooperation, and promoting Indigenous self-determination form the foundation of an equitable approach to resource management. The integration of diverse perspectives and the rejection of colonial-era resource policies allow for a more sustainable future that aligns economic growth with social and environmental responsibility.

6 Conclusion and Outlook

The transition to renewable energy marks a profound shift in global resource dependency, with minerals and metals forming the backbone of decarbonisation strategies. However, this shift brings with it more than just technical and economic challenges—it raises critical questions of governance, equity, and sustainability. As this chapter demonstrates, the mineral intensity of the green energy transition must not obscure the deeper, systemic issues at play. Without fundamental reform, there is a real risk that current trajectories will reproduce the same exploitative colonial patterns that have historically characterised mineral extraction in the Global Majority. A just transition demands more than cleaner technologies; it calls for a departure from extractivist paradigms towards regenerative, community-centred models of resource governance.

Equitable mineral governance hinges on three interconnected imperatives: recognising Indigenous sovereignty and self-determination, embedding sustainability across the supply chain, and dismantling colonial-era structures that continue to shape global resource flows. The principle of Free, Prior, and Informed Consent must move beyond rhetorical endorsement to become a legally binding and enforceable right. While the adoption of circular economy principles and technological innovation is promising, these measures must be embedded within a broader framework of accountability, justice, and inclusive decision-making.

The urgency of climate action requires a recalibration of mineral governance—one that does not repeat historical injustices but instead lays the foundation for a sustainable and equitable future. This moment presents a generational opportunity to reimagine the relationship between natural resources, human societies, and the global economy. Realising that opportunity depends not only on technological progress but on the collective willingness of policymakers, industry leaders, and civil society to embrace a new vision—one in which mineral wealth supports shared prosperity, and sustainability is no longer an aspiration, but a lived reality.

Acknowledgements This publication is part of the Li4Life project. UK participants in Horizon Europe Project—Novel Domestic Battery Grade Lithium Carbonate Value Chain for Green Life—are supported by UKRI Grant No. 10103347 (University of Lincoln). This project has also received funding from the European Union's Horizon 2020 research and innovation programme under grant agreement N° 101137932.

References

Adarve Zuluaga, M., Shortall, N., Stroot, H., Wayand, N., Ruiz, V., Fadel Diop, M., Chester Pagulayan, J., & Emran Hasan, M. (2025, September 24). Unjust transition: Reclaiming the energy future from climate colonialism (Oxfam briefing paper). Oxfam International. https://doi.org/10.21201/2025.000086

Bell, K. (2024). International solidarity for a de-colonised Just Transition: Electric vehicles and lithium in Mexico and Europe. *Contemporary Social Science, 2024*, 1–20.

Bender, A. P., & Bilotta, P. (2020). Circular economy and urban mining: Resource efficiency in the construction sector for sustainable cities. In W. Leal Filho, A. Marisa Azul, L. Brandli, P. G. Özuyar, & T. Wall (Eds.), *Sustainable cities and communities. Encyclopedia of the UN sustainable development goals*. Springer.

Berthet, E., Lavalley, J., Anquetil-Deck, C., et al. (2024). Assessing the social and environmental impacts of critical mineral supply chains for the energy transition in Europe. *Global Environmental Change, 86*, Article 102841.

Bickel, J. P. M., & Mia, I. (2023). Geopolitics and climate change: The significance of south America. In *Survival: August 2023* (pp. 123–138). Routledge.

BP. (2022). *Energy outlook 2022 explores the key uncertainties surrounding the energy transition*. BP Global. bp Energy Outlook 2022

Caron, J., & Asselin, H. (2020). Evaluation of Indigenous employability programs in the Canadian mining industry. *The Extractive Industries and Society, 7*(4), 1424–1437.

Carr-Wilson, S., Pattanayak, S. K., & Weinthal, E. (2024). Critical mineral mining in the energy transition: A systematic review of environmental, social, and governance risks and opportunities. *Energy Research and Social Science, 116*, Article 103672.

Ciftci, M. M., & Lemaire, X. (2023). Deciphering the impacts of 'green energy transition on socio-environmental lithium conflicts: Evidence from Argentina and Chile. *The Extractive Industries and Society, 16*, Article 101373.

CSIS. (2021). *The geopolitics of critical minerals supply chains.* Centre for Strategic & International Studies (CSIS). Available at. https://www.csis.org/analysis/geopolitics-critical-minerals-supply-chains

Diver, S. (2017). Negotiating Indigenous knowledge at the science-policy interface: Insights from the Xáxli'p Community Forest. *Environmental Science and Policy, 73*, 1–11.

Dou, S., Xu, D., Zhu, Y., & Keenan, R. (2023). Critical mineral sustainable supply: Challenges and governance. *Futures, 146*, Article 103101.

European Commission. (2023a). *Grids, the missing link—An EU action plan for grids.* European Commission, COM(2023) 757 final.

European Commission. (2023b). *Establishing a framework for ensuring a secure and sustainable supply of critical raw materials and amending regulations, (EU) 168/2013, (EU) 2018/858, 2018/1724 and (EU) 2019/1020.* European Commission, Brussels, COM(2023) 160 Final.

Ghorbani, Y., Zhang, S. E., Bourdeau, J. E., et al. (2024a). The strategic role of lithium in the green energy transition: Towards an OPEC-style framework for green energy-mineral exporting countries (GEMEC). *Resources Policy, 90*, Article 104737.

Ghorbani, Y., Zhang, S. E., Nwaila, G. T., Bourdeau, J.E., & Rose, D. H. (2024b). Embracing a diverse approach to a globally inclusive green energy transition: Moving beyond decarbonisation and recognising realistic carbon reduction strategies. *Journal of Cleaner Production, 434*, 140414, ISSN 0959-6526.

Gordon, H. S. J., Ross, J. A., Bauer-Armstrong, C., et al. (2023). Integrating indigenous traditional ecological knowledge of land into land management through Indigenous-academic partnerships. *Land Use Policy, 125*, Article 106469.

Hine, A., Gibson, C., & Mayes, R. (2023). Critical minerals: Rethinking extractivism? *Australian Geographer, 54*(3), 233–250.

IEA. (2023a). *Energy technology perspectives 2023.* International Energy Agency, 1–464. Available at: https://www.iea.org/reports/energy-technology-perspectives-2023

IEA. (2023b). *Global energy and climate model.* International Energy Agency, 1–127. Available at: https://www.iea.org/reports/global-energy-and-climate-model

IEA. (2023c). *Tracking clean energy progress 2023*. International Energy Agency. Available at: https://www.iea.org/reports/tracking-clean-energy-progress-2023#overview

IEA. (2024). *Global critical minerals outlook 2024*. International Energy Agency. Available at: https://www.iea.org/reports/global-critical-minerals-outlook-2024

IRENA (International Renewable Energy Agency). (2024). *World energy transitions outlook 2024: 1.5 °C pathway, vol. 1*. International Renewable Energy Agency, 1–176. World Energy Transitions Outlook 2024: 1.5 °C pathway

Jannesar Niri, A., Poelzer, G. A., Zhang, S. E., et al. (2024). Sustainability challenges throughout the electric vehicle battery value chain. *Renewable and Sustainable Energy Reviews, 191*, Article 114176.

Kusniati, R. (2024). Free, prior, and informed consent principles as indigenous peoples' right: Soft law or hard law? *Jambe Law Journal, 7*(1), 169–193.

Loginova, J., Landauer, M., Joona, J., Datta, R., & Joona, T. (2025). Enabling Indigenous-centred decision-making for a just energy transition? Lessons from community consultation and consent in the circumpolar Arctic. *Energy Research and Social Science, 120*, Article 103928.

Manson, A., & Mbenga, B. (2003). 'The richest tribe in Africa': Platinum-mining and the Bafokeng in South Africa's North West Province, 1965–1999. *Journal of Southern African Studies, 29*(1), 25–47.

Mao, Y. (2025). Unveiling the shadows: Reassessing energy security through the lens of petro-violence and green colonialism. *Energy Research and Social Science, 121*, Article 103951.

Mathieu, L., & Mattea, C. (2021). From dirty oil to clean batteries: Batteries vs. oil: A systematic comparison of material requirements. *Transport and Environment, 2021*, 1–75.

Michaux, S. (2021a). *Assessment of the extra capacity required of alternative energy electrical power systems to completely replace fossil fuels*. Geological Survey of Finland (GTK), Report 42/2021, 1-1000.

Michaux, S. (2021b). *The mining of minerals and the limits to growth*. Geological Survey of Finland (GTK), Report 16/2021, 1-73.

Mnwana, S. (2014). Mineral wealth—'In the name of morafe'? Community control in South Africa's 'Platinum Valley.' *Development Southern Africa, 31*(6), 826–842.

Nel, E., & Marais, L. (2024). South Africa's sustainability transition: The case of the mpumalanga province and its coal-dependent communities. In *Rescaling sustainability transitions: Unfolding the spatialities of power relations, governance arrangements, and socio-economic systems* (pp. 247–269). Springer.

Nwaila, G. T., Bourdeau, J. E., Zhang, S. E., et al. (2024). A systematic framework for compilation of critical raw material lists and their importance for South Africa. *Resources Policy, 93*, Article 105045.

O'Donnell, M., Collier, M., Pineda-Pinto, M., et al. (2025). Redefining co-design for social-ecological research and practice: A systematic literature review. *Environmental Science and Policy, 164*, Article 103998.

OECD. (2021). *Due diligence guidance for responsible supply chains of minerals from conflict-affected and high-risk areas* (4th ed.). Organisation for Economic Cooperation and Development Publishing.

Overland, I., Juraev, J., & Vakulchuk, R. (2022). Are renewable energy sources more evenly distributed than fossil fuels? Renew. *Energy, 200*, 379–386.

Palle, A. (2021). Bringing geopolitics to energy transition research. *Energy Research and Social Science, 81*, Article 102233.

Reed, J., Ros-Tonen, M. A. F., Adeyanju, S., et al. (2024). From conflict to collaboration through inclusive landscape governance: Evidence from a contested landscape in Ghana. *Global Environmental Change, 88*, Article 102909.

Russo, A. C., de Melo Loredo, G., & de Tomi, G. F. C. (2024). Small-scale mining as the foundation of sovereignty and mineral security. *The Extractive Industries and Society, 19*, Article 101520.

Sakapaji, S. C., García Molinos, J., Parilova, V., et al. (2024). Navigating legal and regulatory frameworks to achieve the resilience and sustainability of indigenous socioecological systems. *Resources, 13*(4), 56.

See, J., Cuaton, G. P., Placino, P., et al. (2024). From absences to emergences: Foregrounding traditional and Indigenous climate change adaptation knowledges and practices from Fiji, Vietnam, and the Philippines. *World Development, 176*, Article 106503.

Singh, J. T. N. (2010). Governing the extractive sector: The politics of globalisation and copper policy in Chile. *Journal of Critical Global Studies, 3*, 1.

Smith, A., Torres Contreras, G. A., Brisbois, M.-C., et al. (2023). Inclusive innovation in just transitions: The case of smart local energy systems in the UK. *Environmental Innovation and Societal Transitions, 47*, Article 100719.

Sokolova, I., Nwaila, G. T., Ntunka, M. G., Klochkov, S., Michaux, S., Moscardini, E., Toro, L., & Ghorbani, Y. (2025). From abundant resource to critical commodity: Forecasting manganese supply and assessing its sustainability. *Sustainable Materials and Technologies, 44*, Article e01349.

Sovacool, B. K. (2019). The precarious political economy of cobalt: Balancing prosperity, poverty, and brutality in artisanal and industrial mining in the Democratic Republic of Congo. *The Extractive Industries and Society, 6*(3), 915–939.

Sovacool, B. K., Ali, S. H., Bazilian, M., et al. (2020). Sustainable minerals and metals for a low-carbon future. *Science, 367*(6473), 30–33.

Sovacool, B. K., Evensen, D., Kwan, T. A., & Petit, V. (2023). Building a green future: Examining the job creation potential of electricity, heating, and storage in low-carbon buildings. *The Electricity Journal, 36*(5), Article 107274.

Spooren, J., Binnemans, K., Björkmalm, J., et al. (2020). Near-zero-waste processing of low-grade, complex primary ores and secondary raw materials in Europe: Technology development trends. *Resources, Conservation and Recycling, 160*, Article 104919.

Tladi, B., Kambule, N., & Modley, L. A. (2024). Assessing the social and environmental impacts of the just energy transition in Komati, Mpumalanga Province, South Africa. *Energy Research and Social Science, 111*, Article 103489.

Townsend, J., & Roth, R. (2023). Indigenous and decolonial futures: Indigenous Protected and Conserved Areas as potential pathways of reconciliation. *Frontiers in Human Dynamics, 5*, 1286970.

United Nations. (2015). *Transforming our world: the 2030 agenda for sustainable development*. United Nations General Assembly, Resolution adopted by the general Assembly on the 25 September 2015. https://sdgs.un.org/2030agenda

USGS. (2024). *Mineral commodities summaries 2024*. U.S. Geological Survey.

Valizadeh, A., Amirhosseini, M. H., & Ghorbani, Y. (2024). Predictive precision in battery recycling: Unveiling lithium battery recycling potential through machine learning. *Computers and Chemical Engineering, 183*, Article 108623.

Villegas, A., & Scheyder, E. (2023). *Chile plans to nationalize its vast lithium industry*. Reuters. Available at. Chile plans to nationalize its vast lithium industry | Reuters

Watari, T., McLellan, B. C., Giurco, D., Dominish, E., Yamasue, E., & Nansai, K. (2019). Total material requirement for the global energy transition to 2050: A focus on transport and electricity. *Resources, Conservation and Recycling, 148*, 91–103.

Wilson, J. Q. (2021). The politics of regulation. In T. Ferguson & J. Rogers (Eds.), *The political economy: Readings in the politics and economics of American public policy* (pp. 82–103). Routledge.

Woodward, M., Walton, B., Hamilton, J., et al. (2020). *Electric vehicles: Setting a course for 2030*. Deloitte Insights. Available at. Electric vehicle trends | Deloitte Insights

Yao, A., Benson, S. M., & Chueh, W. C. (2025). Critically assessing sodium-ion technology roadmaps and scenarios for techno-economic competitiveness against lithium-ion batteries. *Nature Energy, 10*, 404–416. https://doi.org/10.1038/s41560-024-01701-9

Youdelis, M., Townsend, J., Bhattacharyya, J., et al. (2021). Decolonial conservation: Establishing indigenous protected areas for future generations in the face of extractive capitalism. *Journal of Political Ecology, 28*(1), 990–1022.

Zhang, S. E., Bourdeau, J. E., Nwaila, G. T., & Ghorbani, Y. (2023). Emerging criticality: Unraveling shifting dynamics of the EU's critical raw materials and their implications on Canada and South Africa. *Resources Policy, 86*, Article 104247.

The Challenges of Measuring the Value of Infrastructure from a Gendered Lens

Eurydice Fotopoulou

Abstract Infrastructure is a key component of any economy. It acts as an enabler of inclusion and higher productivity and a catalyst in ensuring access to opportunities and quality of life. It also plays a key role in achieving environmental goals, with sectors such as energy, mining, and transportation infrastructure being a big part of the emissions system. Currently, there is no internationally agreed-upon definition of infrastructure, and different countries produce estimates largely informed by functional interpretations of what can be measured in infrastructure. The dominant definition is informed by the agendas of large economies, focusing on transport, energy, mining, telecommunications, water, waste, and sewerage. Further, there is no agreement of what is "green" infrastructure. As a result, what is measured in National Accounts as infrastructure varies, leading to mismeasurement of economic and social activity, resulting in a patched, biased understanding of development and persistent economic and social inequalities. The lack of agreed definitions offers opportunities and challenges. In this chapter, I assess different definitions of infrastructure and how these may differently affect growth and gender inclusion potential, by virtue of what is included/excluded in the measurement. To contrast this, I present an augmented definition

E. Fotopoulou (✉)
Independent Researcher, London, UK

A. Agunsoye and A. Arntsen (eds.), *Decarbonising and Decolonising Economics*, https://doi.org/10.1007/978-3-032-11972-8_6

of infrastructure, beyond the dominant definition of infrastructure that disadvantages low income and emerging economies, by placing more emphasis on social infrastructure (healthcare, childcare, care of the elderly, education). This has a dual impact: (i) social infrastructure, being human-capital intensive, has a lower carbon footprint than physical investment, and (ii) it can contribute to the decolonialization agenda with the development of awareness and empowerment via education and the long-term effects of productivity. This is examined from a feminist perspective by placing emphasis on why social infrastructure matters, as a vehicle for better access to opportunities and lower social and economic inequality.

Keywords Infrastructure · Inequalities · Gender · Feminist economics

1 Introduction

Continuation of human activity and economic development are evidenced by the infrastructure that remains, often with adaptation and transformation to new circumstances, long after the builders have gone and the disbursement for the work. It is the tangible trace of history after the names of those who built it have been forgotten. Economic development, since antiquity, has been built on a network of roads, ports, bridges, forts and walls, wells, aqueducts, and fortresses, to enable the transportation of goods, bodies, technologies, and ideas. Indeed, colonialization would not have been possible without a parallel investment in the construction of infrastructure that facilitated transfer of resources, some of which is still in use today (for example, the Via Apia Roman road). Trade routes that crossed some of the most climatologically extreme parts of the globe required interventions in the environment to make the crossing of deserts, mountain ranges, and rivers possible. Similarly, because the administration of large regions required quick movement of armies and resources, it necessitated both an effective system of communication (with horse changing stations, for instance) and efficient transportation (ports and roads). All these required recording of this infrastructure so that rulers and administrators could anticipate needs and plan transportation of goods and armies, while maintaining these complex types of infrastructure.

Infrastructure is central in both political economy and political ecology. It acts as an enabler of inclusion and higher productivity, by ensuring access to work, education and healthcare, social and economic opportunities, and broadly a better quality of life. At the same time, infrastructure is a symbol of historical continuity and statehood, with national projects showcasing the ability of a country to modernize and achieve its post-independence vision, for example, with projects that serve as symbols of national self-proclamation instead of improvements to the environment (one could consider the history of the Suez Canal in this light). Infrastructure, or rather the choice of what type of infrastructure is prioritized, represents the dominant culture and is the result of power dynamics. Road networks imply an outward-looking culture, interested in trade and exchange, while fortresses may imply awareness of violence and concern for safety by a warring state. This chapter gives a snapshot of how infrastructure can be understood and situated in the environment, to bring in the human element from a gendered lens.

Power dynamics underpin the value and role of infrastructure in global decolonialization and diversification attempts. Over time, infrastructure has shaped and has been shaped by the tensions between labor and capital, but also between humans and the environment. The tensions between labor and capital have been documented extensively elsewhere, especially in the context of slavery, exploitation, and discrimination in the construction sector in several countries (Yanochik et al., 2003; Annian, 2006; Hedwards et al., 2017; Chandran & Chacko, 2017; Akhtar, 2021; Alzoubi et al., 2023, among others). The tensions between humans and the environment, more specifically those that have led to environmental degradation and destruction, have also been examined by a large body of literature, from the perspective of internal colonialism, carbon colonialism, extractivism, with climate and energy coloniality proliferating within discussions on climate-change mitigation and "green" infrastructural development (Dunlap, 2023; De Onís, 2018; Andreucci & Zografos, 2022; Sultana, 2022). Alkhalili et al. (2023) demonstrate how the "investments in renewable energy are yet another extension of a logic of colonial extractivism which produces infrastructures that cause harm to the communities, nature, political and cultural sovereignty" of people (p. 2). The authors argue that while wind energy is often presented as a solution to the climate crisis, it can also perpetuate colonial patterns of exploitation. For instance, such projects can have harmful impacts on communities already striving for self-determination, as their lands and resources are appropriated for energy production. This approach, rooted in a colonial mindset, treats the natural environment merely as a source of profit for governments, corporations, and development agencies, echoing historical patterns of extraction and accumulation, as Núñez et al. (2022), for example, investigate in the case of Patagonia. The notion of internal colonialism highlights how the racialized political, economic, environmental, and social relations that structured colonized territories persist, even after their formal independence (Casanova, 2005; Saldívar, 2014). Consequently, what infrastructure is being built can replicate attitudes of the colonial past, or attitudes of the metropole (especially with emphasis on extractive and energy infrastructure), implying obstinate dependence.

Considering infrastructure separately from the environment (and the tensions around it) is not possible, neither in practice, nor in policy. The power of infrastructure in shaping the future and preserving the memory of the past was part of the early consultations upon the conclusion of Millenium Development Goals and the ensuing Sustainable Development Goals (SDG). Infrastructure is 1 of 17 sustainable development goals proposed by the United Nations and is a key consideration for countries seeking sustainable growth and thus shape their future in a more environmentally friendly way. Additionally, there are six more goals relating directly to the environment.[1] Other goals, more encompassing and in the intersection of the two—environment and infrastructure—such as SDG 11 (Sustainable Cities and Communities) and SDG 9 (Industry, Innovation, and Infrastructure)—include environmental aspects related to urbanization, infrastructure, and industrial activities that impact the environment. Here, emphasis is placed on the ways industrial activity can be improved by smart infrastructure (i.e., sensor systems, etc.).[2] By design, the SDGs serve as the program labels under which funds for development can be allocated. Since the adoption of the SDGs there has been notable progress in expanding infrastructure and related services, but significant gaps remain, especially in rural areas, low-income countries, and fragile and conflict-affected states. The IMF estimated that an additional annual

[1] These are: SDG 6: Clean Water and Sanitation, SDG 7: Affordable and Clean Energy, SDG 12: Responsible Consumption and Production, SDG 13: Climate Action, SDG 14: Life Below Water, SDG 15: Life on Land. For a comprehensive list of the SDG and their sub-components, please see: https://sdgs.un.org/goals.

[2] Smart infrastructure and how it can replicate bias to sustain and even increase inequality is beyond the scope of this paper.

spending of about US$1.4 trillion will be needed for investment in roads, electricity networks, and water and sanitation facilities in low-income countries and emerging economies to make meaningful progress toward SDGs in these areas (Gaspar et al., 2019).

Infrastructure availability, quality, and condition impact population groups differently because of their respective roles, responsibilities, and vulnerabilities. Thus, although the SDG on gender equality does not explicitly refer to infrastructure, infrastructure is a prerequisite for the delivery of sustainable growth in an inclusive way for women. More specifically, SDG 5 addresses various aspects of gender inequality, including ending discrimination and violence against women, ensuring equal participation in decision-making processes, and guaranteeing equal access to education, healthcare, and economic opportunities. Gender is a cross-cutting issue, relevant to poverty and inequality reduction broadly (SDG 1, 8, 10), as well as those SDGs that target improvements in healthcare and educational outcome. Delivery of these goals for women will be impossible without the construction and maintenance of schools, clinics, and electricity. How can women have equality if they spend hours fetching water because there is no water distribution system? How can girls be educated when they spend more time than boys collecting firewood because they have no other source of energy? How can women participate more in the labor market, if they do not have access to affordable and safe public transportation? How can women be in control of their reproductive rights, if they have no access to a clinic?

Therefore, measuring the value of infrastructure in an economy is crucial because it can indicate the potential the economy has to grow, it can reduce inequalities, and signal whether development is done in a way that is not environmentally detrimental. What do we currently measure though? How good is our measurement of infrastructure?

In the following sections, I will attempt to provide a possible answer to these questions. Initially, I outline definitions in use by different countries. Subsequently, I assess the usefulness of these definitions for the purposes of gender inclusivity and environmental sustainability. Thirdly, I discuss the ways the current measurement of infrastructure impacts women. In the final section of this chapter, I propose alternative ways of thinking, as well as mention work currently underway to improve future measurement of infrastructure. These include expanding on the role of social infrastructure (healthcare, childcare, care of the elderly, education) as a low-carbon path to development. Simultaneously, emphasis on accessible social infrastructure can lead to more equitable societies that are consciously empowered to break free from colonial forms of dependence in the long run.

2 Definitions of Infrastructure

Naturally, when measuring anything at a macroeconomic level, the first point of reference is usually internationally agreed standards to ensure comparability and consistency in economic statistics across countries. The System of National Accounts (SNA) 2008[3] has been the United Nations framework that lays out measurement of most types of economic activity that are included in countries' national accounts. In this section, I deliberate on how infrastructure is defined in the SNA, and debate the notion of "green" infrastructure within existing frameworks and practice.

Infrastructure in the SNA 2008 is measured as part of fixed assets, and it contributes to Gross Fixed Capital Formation (GFCF). It is calculated primarily through the expenditure approach, with a focus on acquisition costs and improvements to existing assets. More specifically, infrastructure assets are classified under fixed assets, which refer to tangible or intangible assets used repeatedly or continuously in production processes for more than one year. Infrastructure investment contributes to GFCF, which is a key component of the national accounts. GFCF measures the net increase in the stock of fixed assets in an economy during a particular period. It includes (a) the acquisition of new fixed assets (construction of new infrastructure), and (b) major improvements or additions to existing fixed assets (for example, the expansion or modernization of infrastructure). The SNA 2008 is used by all advanced economies and most emerging economies and low-income countries; those that have not fully applied it are gradually moving towards it. Notably, it forms the basis of reporting for all UN bodies and international organizations, advanced economies, as well as Brazil, India, China, South Africa, Mexico, Vietnam, Turkey, Argentina, and Nigeria, among others.

The process typically considers the following. Infrastructure investment is measured using the expenditure approach, in other words, recording the actual expenditures incurred in acquiring, constructing, or improving

[3] Available here: https://unstats.un.org/unsd/nationalaccount/docs/sna2008.pdf.

infrastructure assets. These expenditures include costs related to activities that span the entirety of the asset, such as planning, design, construction, and installation. The value of infrastructure assets is recorded at their acquisition or production cost, which includes all costs necessary to bring the infrastructure asset into its intended condition and location for use. Similarly to all assets that contribute to capital formation, infrastructure assets are subject to depreciation, which reflects the gradual loss in value over time due to wear and tear, obsolescence, or other factors (for example, damage from natural disasters, war damage, etc.). Depreciation is deducted from gross fixed capital formation to calculate net fixed capital formation, which represents the net addition to the capital stock. In the case of infrastructure, estimation of depreciation is quite complex, first, because infrastructure assets can have shared national ownership and be subject to different ways of maintenance, and second, the same type of asset (e.g., a road) may have been constructed with more advance engineering standards or materials at different parts, or it may have different traffic intensity and volume at different sections.

A careful reader will notice that the statistical manual focusses on investment in infrastructure, without saying much about "what" infrastructure is. This is because there is no internationally agreed-upon definition on what infrastructure is. Infrastructure investments are classified according to the type of asset by industrial category (for instance, transportation, communication, energy) and the economic sector in which they are used. Most advanced countries use a functional definition, based on their ability to identify the relevant categories in data, and include: (1) transportation: roads and highways, bridges, tunnels, railways, airports, ports, and harbors, (2) communication: telecommunications networks (e.g., telephone lines, cellular networks), broadcasting networks (e.g., radio and television transmission infrastructure), (3) energy: power generation facilities (e.g., power plants, wind farms, solar farms), transmission and distribution networks (e.g., electricity grids, natural gas pipelines), (4) water and sewerage: water supply systems (e.g., dams, reservoirs, water treatment plants), sewerage and drainage systems, (5) mining, and (6) usually a catch-all "other" category that may include public buildings and facilities (e.g., government offices, schools, hospitals), recreational and cultural facilities (e.g., parks, museums, sports complexes), public lighting systems, public space infrastructure, etc.

The lack of definition of a formal infrastructure is further enmeshed with the lack of clarity around what "green" infrastructure is. Conceptually, "green" infrastructure may refer to infrastructure projects that do not add to the carbon footprint of an activity, or that contribute to the improvement of the quality of the environment, or that align with a net zero greenhouse gas emissions target. It may also be related to infrastructure projects that are made with specific materials or following a specific process. Therefore the shorthand "green" tends to refer to carbon-neutral processes. The European Union defines it as "a strategically planned network of natural and semi-natural areas with other environmental features, designed and managed to deliver a wide range of ecosystem services, while also enhancing biodiversity[4]". Such services include, for example, water purification (via soil filtering), improving air quality (by planting trees near dense traffic areas as a means of decarbonization), providing space for recreation (parks, playgrounds, open air sports grounds), as well as helping with climate mitigation and adaptation. Grabowski et al. (2022) argue that in the USA city planning authorities often fail to explicitly define "green infrastructure" and at the time of publication, official discource in the USA is moving away from any climate-relevant terminology. Even when they do, stormwater concepts of "green" infrastructure (flood prevention structures) are much more prevalent than landscape or integrative concepts and can vary widely and significantly, often excluding parks and larger urban green spaces in favor of smaller engineered facilities. These definitions are based on preservation of biodiversity, rather than redesign of dense and deprived urban areas, for example, which may be needed in developing countries. Despite the existence of SDGs relating to the environment, just like with the case of infrastructure, the lack of clarity around "green" infrastructure necessitates the use of quotation marks throughout this chapter and in public discourse.[5] As a result, policy based on these incomplete notions may also be incomplete, and as a result, only partially addressing issues around the environment.

[4] For more on the European environmental policy, please see: https://environment.ec.europa.eu/topics/nature-and-biodiversity/green-infrastructure_en.

[5] Perhaps the characterization "low-carbon" may be more appropriate in same cases.

3 Assessment of the Definitions of Infrastructure

In general, the advantage of this functional classification-as-definition is that it allows for detailed analysis of investment patterns and economic activities across different major sectors of the economy and gives the flexibility to countries to include what they deem a necessary part of infrastructure, according to their needs. There are two main disadvantages though. The first is that without a common definition, international comparisons are not satisfactory, as they may contain broadly similar but qualitatively distinct elements. For instance, due to characteristics specific to a terrain, the same investment may not yield the same structure. To illustrate this, one may consider the difference in building a road on a rocky mountain in high altitude, as opposed to building a road in valley that is prone to flooding. In both cases the investment will be recorded as investment in ***building a road***, but the work required to construct and maintain the roads is different (e.g., in the former, it is required to blast rock and build structures that would not collapse with the first avalanche or crack under extreme cold, and in the latter to create a drainage system, etc.). To resolve this, there are currently international efforts underway to develop a common, standard definition of infrastructure, which are articulated in the latest update of the SNA. This includes, often, transportation, communications and information, energy and utilities, water, and mining. The second disadvantage is that some infrastructure categories are either left out, such as prisons, student accommodation, and care homes for the elderly, or aggregated. The omissions may lead to an underestimation of the need for certain types of investment or imply that there is already sufficient investment in some categories because the figures have been summed up with other irrelevant/archaic categories to the interests of the current demographic.

The last point is relevant to the last category in the classification, ironically named "other". This can include education and healthcare facilities, usually aggregated with infrastructure that has entirely different function in daily economic activity, as well as impact on productivity and well-being, such as correctional infrastructure. Education and healthcare are necessary conditions to reduce inequality, especially gender inequality, as they provide access to key services to close gender gaps and achieve the SDGs. Education and healthcare facilities may be referred to as social infrastructure, because of their role in supporting community well-being. Identifying investment in these categories is often challenging in public financial accounts (and there is limited private investment in these) because of complex administration structures, especially when there are multiple sources of government funding (for example central-local, state-federal, etc.).

Regarding categories that are left out, a glaring example is informal infrastructure, admittedly, one of the most challenging aspects of infrastructure. Mbembe and Nuttal (2004) suggest that formally planned infrastructure, authorized, and built by the government and private sector, exists in relationship to informal temporary, ad-hoc infrastructures, such as slums or informal energy networks. This notion of incremental, informal infrastructures has been considered in more detail by Simone (2008, 2011) and McFarlane (2011), who analyze the ways by which urban dwellers seek to improve their habitat conditions through multiple and unfolding encounters with urban infrastructural configurations. While government investment may provide new or improved infrastructural conditions, the role of urban dwellers in generating new, organic, urban spaces cannot be underestimated, especially when it is the outcome of innovation for survival. Inattention to non-formal activities undertaken by the urban poor is a consistent gap in the study of post-colonial urbanization (Pieterse, 2008). Consequently, any attempt to measure infrastructure, because precisely it ignores some of the most vulnerable populations, without informal infrastructure, will inadvertently miss those who may benefit the most from it.

Statistical definitions fail to capture additional, historically and culturally charged aspects of any physical structure. Different types of infrastructure have symbolic value beyond their economic value, as already mentioned, such as national self-proclamation. Often mega-projects may be prioritized as they can be used to enhance national pride and modern monuments of economic might and promise, potentially making up for the monuments of past exploitation. For example, according to Enns and Bersaglio (2020), colonial administrations in East Africa prioritized infrastructure development for the extraction, production, and movement of commodities through their territories. Nowadays, governments in East Africa are pursuing large-scale infrastructure programs that trace the colonial past geographically, such as the Lamu Port-South Sudan-Ethiopia Transport (LAPSSET) Corridor in Kenya. In this sense, infrastructure development in both the colonial and post-independence eras is associated with the organization of space to facilitate the extroversion of East African economies. However, today's mega-infrastructure projects depart from the past in certain ways. Perhaps the most visible differences are the new modes of infrastructure being constructed along pre-existing infrastructure routes. These infrastructure projects are meant to speed up movement and diminish distance, reducing the cost of the movement of commodities and accelerating production (Danyluk, 2018). As such, the projects reflect the aspiration to reduce the gap between advanced and less developed countries, but they are beyond the scope of "measurable".

4 Infrastructure and Women

Why do roads, electricity, schools, and clean running water matter more for women? In this section, I look at gender-differentiated impacts of infrastructure investments in transportation, regular access to electricity, water and sanitation, and information and communications technology (ICT), informed by the role of women as primary caregivers, drawing heavily from a comprehensive review by Britt and Egerer (2024). I also revisit the known benefits of access to healthcare and education for women. The narrative that follows shows that infrastructure can create barriers to women, preventing them from accessing opportunities such as going to school, to work, or saving time when doing their daily chores. What is more, not only does it block opportunities, but it may create obstacles that can be sources of fear for women. I also intimate the different environmental impact of different types of infrastructure and how these affect women: their safety, their integrity, their health, their potential, and their access to opportunities.

Investments in roads and transportation can yield benefits for all. Nonetheless, women have distinct travel patterns, perceptions of threats, financial constraints, and safety considerations that significantly influence their mobility and choice of transportation. According to Rezenberg and Fay (2019), over a billion people reside more than two kilometers away from an all-season road, while many others face restricted access to employment and educational opportunities due to transport unavailability or high costs. Lei et al. (2019) report that in rural India, better road access and increased bus frequency have bolstered non-agricultural employment prospects for both genders, with women's participation rates exceeding those of men, particularly in communities where more egalitarian gender norms exist. Numerous studies underscore how travel behaviors of women and men mirror gender-specific roles, such as caregiving which is seen primarily as a woman's responsibility. Women tend to use cars less and depend more on public transport (arguably a lower carbon emission option compared to private cars) due to financial necessity, resulting in lower rates of cycling (which is a "green" mode of transportation) and higher incidences of trip-chaining—taking multiple short trips with stops at various destinations, often during non-peak hours, and more often on foot. Security perceptions and the fear of sexual harassment repeatedly compel women to modify travel plans, restricting their freedom of movement (Coppola & Silvestri, 2021, Dominguez Gonzales et al., 2020) and consequently may restrict their access to opportunities that would require regular transportation during peak times. This comes with a high psychological cost, with approximately 80% of women reporting anxiety about harassment in public spaces, contributing to diminished labor force participation in low-income countries by 16.5% (Gonzales Carvajal & Meehmood Alam, 2018). This complex picture of the usage of transportation infrastructure by women indicates that, in general, women could use more types of transportation with a lower carbon footprint, under the right circumstances.

Consequently, measures such as better street lighting and stronger/enforceable public transport safety protocols are fundamental for women's mobility and economic empowerment, by facilitating safer transportation options for commuting. Remote work, which has become more common during the Covid-19 pandemic and could be a solution under certain conditions, has had a mixed impact on the ability of women to access opportunities (Angelucci et al., 2020; Fan & Moen, 2022; Sandoval-Reyes et al., 2021; Thomas, 2021), with some findings indicating that it reduced their independence (Shen & Zamani, 2024).

Considering work, one should not disregard women's work within the household, where infrastructure that reaches homes could be transformative for women's lives, too. For example, access to reliable and affordable electricity and labor-saving appliances in households can alleviate women's domestic workloads, possibly liberating time for other productive endeavors. On average, women and girls spend 18 hours every week and travel considerable distances to gather biomass for cooking (UN Women, 2018). According to UN Women (2020), 733 million people lacked access to electricity, with 2.4 billion reliant on inefficient and polluting energy sources for cooking, such as wood, dung, and crop residues. Given that cooking and other household tasks are undertaken mostly by women and girls, they are disproportionately affected by indoor air pollution from unclean combustible fuels used for cooking. Samad and Zhang (2019) claim that access to electricity increases not only women's employment, but also their freedom of movement and ability to participate in socio-political activities. Financing remains a major obstacle to achieving universal electricity access, with many projects dependent on public support (UN Women, 2022). According to the 2022 Tracking SDG 7 Progress Report, global access to electricity increased from 83% in 2010 to 91% in 2020, benefiting approximately 1.3 billion people. Projections from the International Energy Agency (IEA, 2023) suggest that achieving universal electricity access by 2030 will necessitate annual investments exceeding US$35 billion. The energy mix, though, and its impact on the environment remains a challenge.

As a result, investment in electricity generation and distribution remains key. However, given the large proportion of the global population that resides in parts of the world with largely informal or non-existent electricity networks, the way electricity infrastructure is measured may require a creative rethink, with the use of big data (e.g., using satellite imagery to trace informal networks, or greenhouse gas emissions). There is also a need for cleaner forms of energy—a process that has already started with renewable energy generation absorbing 93% of total private infrastructure investment in the world.[6] As "greener" forms of energy production become more prevalent, there are certainly opportunities to consider how gender dynamics can be improved through their introduction. Osunmuyiwa and Ahlborg (2022) found that depending on new energy and existing power structures has the potential to disrupt community gender hierarchies. Investigating women's entrepreneurship in Tanzania, they found that the introduction of small-scale renewable energy systems, contrary to large-scale flagship projects, could encourage women entrepreneurs to expand their businesses, with access to more affordable energy. "Green" energy generation remains challenging to track in the entire supply chain, but the simple replacement

[6] Global Infrastructure Hub. Accessed 13 July 2024, available at: https://www.gihub.org/infrastructure-monitor/insights/private-investment-must-look-beyond-renewables-to-reach-net-zero/.

of biomass-fueled kitchens with solar ones, for instance, can bring not only environmental benefits but non-negligible female health benefits.

Another type of essential infrastructure that affects women relates to hygiene and sanitation provision. While basic water, sanitation and hygiene coverage has increased in the twenty-first century, large inequalities remain in accessibility, availability, and quality. According to estimates by the World Health Organisation (WHO, 2022), about 2 billion people do not have access to safe water services, and at least 733 million people live in areas under high and critical levels of water stress, where the need for safe and usable water is greater than the supply. In addition to this, meeting drinking water, sanitation, and hygiene targets by 2030 will need speeding up the pace of progress and would save 829,000 lives annually (WHO, 2022). Globally, women and girls are disproportionately responsible for collecting and managing water use in their households. A 2017 WHO report, drawing from the experience of women in 61 countries, suggests that women and girls are responsible for water collection in 8 out of 10 households where water is not available at home (WHO, 2017). In many cases, this means that women and girls have to walk for miles to retrieve water, exposing them to physical risks and harm, including gender-based violence (UN Women, 2022). These numbers are even more concerning in Africa, according to UNICEF (2022) where 411 million people lack basic drinking water service, 779 million lack basic sanitation services and 839 million lack basic hygiene services. Inadequate hygiene and sanitation services impact everyone, with additional negative implications for the health, safety, mobility, and educational and economic opportunities of women and girls. Apart from the direct impact this may have on women's and girls' own health and well-being, due to their caring responsibilities in the household, lack of access to water and sanitation facilities can indirectly increase the care burden, when this could have been prevented. The lack of water, hygiene and sanitation infrastructure due to their impact on human health can decrease productivity, as well as reduce educational, social, and economic opportunities (e.g., missing school during menstruation). In some countries, public buildings, including schools and health centers, lack toilets that are private, safe, and sanitary, and there is evidence that inadequate water and sanitation facilities in schools negatively impacts attendance, especially among girls reaching puberty (UNICEF, 2021). Such infrastructure may also exist informally, which can compound the negative impact on women's health (for example infections from open sewers). In any case, such missing or informal infrastructure is not measured, leading to infrastructure deserts on paper, which could be occasionally an advantage, because certain areas may be prioritized for development.

Digital infrastructure is increasingly being added to the list of electricity, water and sanitation as essential infrastructure. Although digital connectivity is expanding globally, approximately 2.6 billion people remain offline in 2023 (ITU, 2023). It is encouraging that growth in internet connectivity remains the strongest in low-income countries, where data indicate that internet users increased by about 17% over the past year (ITU, 2023). However, the digital gender gap in low-income countries remains significant with no evidence of narrowing. In 2023, 44% of the male population in low-income countries was online, increasing from 31% in 2019. That is 9 percentage points more than the share among the female population (35%), which experienced an increase of only 3 percentage points since 2019 (ITU, 2023). The gender gap for mobile phone ownership remains wide, too. In 2023, 67% of men (aged ten and above) in low-income countries owned a mobile phone compared with 58% of women. This demonstrates clearly that investment in digital infrastructure benefits men more than women, even though, admittedly, less than one-third of individuals are connected to the internet in these countries and this goes hand-in-hand with the need to develop digital skills. Over 230 million jobs in Sub-Saharan Africa will require digital skills by 2030 (IFC, 2021). However, in practice this is a challenge because the division of subjects, particularly in STEM education—which enhances digital skills and promotes ICT-related job opportunities—is perpetuating gender gaps in these fields. For instance, only 7% of girls in upper secondary education (compared to 18% of boys) in 34 developing countries opted for STEM majors, disadvantaging women and girls in ICT even more (ILO, 2018). Further, investment in digital infrastructure does not imply affordability of connectivity. As women tend to have lower incomes than men globally, the gender gap in internet use, mobile phone subscription, and mobile phone ownership is impacted by other factors beyond existing infrastructure. The Alliance for Affordable Internet in 2021 estimated that increasing the digital inclusion of women and girls by 2025 could boost global GDP by US$524 billion (Alliance for Affordable Internet, 2021). Lack of connectivity can lead to a spiral of exclusion, not only from access to employment opportunities (like remote work), limiting financial resource access and control. Financial technology companies enable increased financial inclusion among the unbanked, especially in more remote places, where there are no bank branches or money transfer stations, and among women, who may not be always able to visit a bank on their own, due to cultural constraints. This can bring better control over savings and income, with potential multiplier effects in social benefits over time, such as in education, public health, agriculture, and women's access to and control over income.

Additionally, gender equality in internet and mobile phone access and improving digital literacy are part of SDG 5, which focuses on achieving gender equality pledges in the use of ICTs to "promote the empowerment of women" (Target 5b). Building and sustaining high-quality ICT infrastructure and networks typically demands significant government investment to ensure equitable coverage, because private companies tend to engage primarily in areas with a positive return on investment, such as urban or densely populated regions. Besides this consideration, structures that are complementary to ICT infrastructure, such as data centers, are found to be quite resource intensive, especially in terms of using scarce water resources to cool down computers, and energy to power them. According to the IEA (2023), energy use in data centers and high-performance computing is undergoing explosive growth, consumed up to 2% of the global electricity supply in 2021, while emitting 1% of energy-related greenhouse gas emissions in 2023. Identifying data centers separately from other structures in infrastructure measurement is a demanding exercise, because they are often considered critical or commercially sensitive infrastructure, and their location (or even existence) is not disclosed, making this another potential case of missing or undermeasured infrastructure. Therefore, striking a balance in measuring ICT infrastructure is challenging, especially given the policy pressures to invest in it to close gender and income gaps. The environmental cost may not be immediately obvious, affecting men and women disproportionately as we saw previously too, when considering sanitation and hygiene.

Social infrastructure, such as healthcare and education facilities, is well-documented elsewhere as a key element in the reduction of poverty and the closing of gender gaps, with long-term effects on productivity and growth (Onaran et al., 2022; Small & van der Meulen Rodgers, 2023). There is a large body of literature arguing that completed basic education of women has been associated with better health of young children (Lakshman et al., 2013), lower fertility rates (Chicoine, 2021), but also with increases in employment opportunities (Klasen & Lamanna, 2009), skills, and economic growth (Mammen & Paxson, 2000; Jorgenson &

Fraumeni, 2020). To materialize, these benefits require investment in healthcare and education infrastructure, such as clinics, schools, and climate-change resistant classrooms (Ansong et al., 2018), with evidence that the difference in regional academic performance is conditional on the infrastructure inequality in some countries, such as Ghana and Tanzania (Agyei et al., 2024; Zacharia, 2014). Social infrastructure may not be entirely distinct from ICT infrastructure, as it contributes to the development of the necessary digital skills, and the access to water, sanitation, and hygiene infrastructures, which are necessary conditions for health outcomes. In this context, as previously mentioned, there might be health or education infrastructure that prevents women from participating in education or accessing healthcare due to lack of sanitation facilities, especially during menstruation. Although there is limited evidence of the emissions of healthcare and education facilities in low-income countries, they are generally thought of as less energy intensive as other types of infrastructure. Their emissions naturally depend on the type of energy used to operate. The nature of the service delivered is care/knowledge intensive and depends on the available human capital. Thus, it is not unlikely that the output of this type of investment is "greener" and can offer long-term productivity returns (Onaran et al., 2022), alongside empowerment that may arise due to higher human capital.

5 Need for an Augmented Definition

So far, I have endeavored to present how investment in different types of infrastructure can impact women in a different way, from energy generation projects to access to clean water and hygiene facilities in healthcare and education infrastructure. I also pointed out that ICT infrastructure, which is flourishing to accelerate the digital convergence between advanced economies and less-developed ones, requires careful planning due to its cross-cutting services and potential strain on the environment. Although the results in some cases are inconclusive, planning and investing in the right type of infrastructure can be particularly impactful in achieving sustainable growth that is inclusive and equitable. This in turn requires a clear understanding of what infrastructure assets are included in the measurement and what is their carbon profile in the long run, for sustainable development.

To achieve this, what needs to be addressed is the establishment of a consensus on the definition of infrastructure, in a way that incorporates the post-colonial experience of countries that aspire to grow by extending infrastructure in an environmentally sustainable way. This may require the acknowledgment that asset value and, more importantly, infrastructure asset lives will have to be calculated not only with climate change in mind, but their ability to include or exclude populations from opportunities and services. Further, informal infrastructure should become visible in national accounts by becoming part of the definition of infrastructure, because it has the same function as formal infrastructure by providing services such as shelter, transportation, and access to energy, and it can qualify for classification as a fixed asset, despite not being part of the formal urban plan. This can be done by proxy measurement, or by embracing alternative data sources, such as satellite data (nightlight, carbon dioxide, nitrogen dioxide, vegetation cover, etc.) to identify informal structures, like dirt roads, unpaved runways, informal energy networks.

Therefore, an augmented, international agreed and relevant definition of infrastructure, in addition to common categories of infrastructure, for the purposes of good measurement should include social infrastructure as a separate category, accommodate for the inclusion of informal infrastructure, and the inclusion of a forward-looking definition of ICT infrastructure assets. The former two would be particularly relevant for gender-aware urban planning, while the latter could lead to legislated disclosure (respecting confidentiality where necessary) of infrastructure assets, such as data centers, that may have significant environmental impact.

6 Conclusion

This chapter showcases that the measurement of human constructions is incomplete, even though the physical and spatial evidence will remain as testament of the power dynamics that shaped it, including colonial, gender, or environmental dynamics. Besides my proposition for an augmented definition of infrastructure, I offer a few suggestions on how measurement of infrastructure can be improved.

A practical way of improving measurement is by adding assessments of gender inclusion and gendered impacts of infrastructure, apart from the emerging practice of including the environmental impact, especially in projects that affect traditional structures. The World Bank (2010) suggests six valuable assessment criteria: (1) consultation with women to understand the impact of the infrastructure on them, (2) whether a gender analysis was conducted in the context of social or environmental assessments or resettlement action planning, (3) whether gender equality goals were included as part of the project development objectives, (4) gender-responsive design, including provisions for potential employment opportunities for women in the project, (5) whether there is earmarking for targeted gender activities and plan in the budget, and (6) whether the project specifically monitored gender-responsive indicators as the project progressed. Inclusion of these considerations may help national statisticians, investors, and planners to record more accurately the value of infrastructure assets, by accounting for effects that were previously missing. Certainly, a determined visionary could extend these propositions to decolonize infrastructure, for example by accounting for indigenous populations' interests and needs, as in the case of New Zealand.

If one looks at human infrastructure from the troposphere, they may not be able to see the inequality it may have caused or reduced, or its use to extract, exploit, and constrain, but they may be able to see desertification and pollution. Better measurement of infrastructure could lead to a higher degree of accountability and more responsible and inclusive policies, better urban planning, and the delivery services that help all achieve their potential, beyond the SDGs.

References

Agyei, E. A., Annim, S. K., Acquah, B. Y. S., Sebu, J., & Agyei, S. K. (2024). Education infrastructure inequality and academic performance in Ghana. *Heliyon*. Retrieved October 8, 2024, from https://www.cell.com/heliyon/fulltext/S2405-8440(24)10072-2?_returnURL=https%3A%2F%2Flinkinghub.elsevier.com%2Fretrieve%2Fpii%2FS2405844024100722%3Fshowall%3Dtrue

Akhtar, Z. (2021). Eastern European workers: Exploitation in the construction industry and enforcement by regulatory agencies. *Construction Law International, 16*(1), 42–45.

Alkhalili, A., Bader, A., & Mkhize, N. (2023). The enduring coloniality of ecological modernization: Wind energy development in occupied Western Sahara and the occupied Syrian Golan Heights. *Environmental Science and Policy*.

Alliance for Affordable Internet. (2021). *The costs of exclusion: Economic consequences of the digital gender gap*. Web Foundation. https://a4ai.org/research/the-costs-of-exclusion

Alzoubi, Y., Locatelli, G., & Sainati, T. (2023). The ugly side of construction: Modern slavery in the 2022 FIFA World Cup program. *Construction Management and Economics, 42*(5), 412–430.

Andreucci, D., & Zografos, C. (2022). Between improvement and sacrifice: Othering and the (bio) political ecology of climate change. *Political Geography, 92*, Article 102512.

Angelucci, M., Angrisani, M., Bennett, D. M., Kapteyn, A., & Schaner, S. G. (2020). *Remote work and the heterogeneous impact of COVID-19 on employment and health (No. w27749)*. National Bureau of Economic Research.

Annian, H. (2006). *The silent spikes: Chinese laborers and the construction of North American railroads*. 中信出版社.

Ansong, D., Renwick, C. B., Okumu, M., Ansong, E., & Wabwire, C. J. (2018). Gendered geographical inequalities in junior high school enrollment: Do infrastructure, human, and financial resources matter? *Journal of Economic Studies, 45*(2), 411–425.

Britt, C., & Egerer, D. (2024). Exploring the role of public expenditure in advancing female economic empowerment and gender equality. *Gender and Development*.

Casanova, P. G. (2005). The Zapatista "caracoles": Networks of resistance and autonomy. *Socialism and Democracy, 19*(3), 79–92.

Chandran, A., & Chacko, C. M. (2017). Exploitation of in-migrant construction workers in Kerala: A case study. *South Asian Journal of Infrastructure Research and Finance, 4*(1), 37–50.

Chicoine, L. (2021). Free primary education, fertility, and women's access to the labor market: Evidence from Ethiopia. *The World Bank Economic Review, 35*(2), 480–498.

Coppola, P., & Silvestri, F. (2021). Gender inequality in safety and security perceptions in railway stations. *Sustainability, 13*(7), Article 4007.

Danyluk, M. (2018). Capital's logistical fix: Accumulation, globalization, and the survival of capitalism. *Environment and Planning D: Society and Space, 36*(4), 630–647.

De Onís, C. M. (2018). Energy colonialism powers the ongoing unnatural disaster in Puerto Rico. *Frontiers in Communication, 3*, 2.

Dominguez Gonzalez, K., Machado, A. L., Bianchi Alves, B., Raffo, V., Guerrero, S., & Portabales, I. (2020). Why does she move? A study of women's mobility in Latin American Cities. *World Bank.*

Dunlap, A. (2023). The green economy as counterinsurgency, or the ontological power affirming permanent ecological catastrophe. *Environmental Science and Policy, 139*, 39–50.

Enns, C., & Bersaglio, B. (2020). On the coloniality of "new" mega-infrastructure projects in East Africa. *Antipode, 52*(1), 101–123.

Fan, W., & Moen, P. (2022). Working more, less, or the same during COVID-19? A mixed-method, intersectional analysis of remote workers. *Work and Occupations, 49*(2), 143–186.

Gaspar, V., et al. (2019). Fiscal policy and development: Human, social and physical investment for the SDGs. *IMF Staff Discussion Note*, 19(3).

Gonzalez Carvajal, K., & Meehmood Alam M. (2018). Transport is not gender-neutral. *Transport for Development*. World Bank.

Grabowski, Z. J., McPhearson, T., Matsler, A. M., Groffman, P., & Pickett, S. T. (2022). What is green infrastructure? A study of definitions in US city planning. *Frontiers in Ecology and the Environment, 20*(3), 152–160.

Hedwards, B., Andrevski, H., & Bricknell, S. (2017). Labour exploitation in the Australian construction industry: Risks and protections for temporary migrant workers. *Australian Institute of Criminology.*

International Energy Agency. (2023). *Data centres and data transmission networks.*

International Finance Corporation. (2021). *Women and e-commerce in Africa.* International Finance Corporation.

International Labour Organization. (2018). *World employment and social outlook 2018: Greening with jobs.*

International Telecommunication Union. (2023). *Measuring digital development: Facts and figures 2023.* United Nations.

Jorgenson, D. W., & Fraumeni, B. M. (2020). Investment in education and US economic growth. In *The US savings challenge* (pp. 114–149). Routledge.

Klasen, S., & Lamanna, F. (2009). The impact of gender inequality in education and employment on economic growth: New evidence for a panel of countries. *Feminist Economics, 15*(3), 91–132.

Lakshman, R., Zhang, J., Zhang, J., Koch, F. S., Marcus, C., Ludvigsson, J., Ong, K. K., & Sobko, T. (2013). Higher maternal education is associated with favourable growth of young children in different countries. *J Epidemiol Community Health, 67*(7), 595–602.

Lei, L., Desai, S., & Vanneman, R. (2019). The impact of transportation infrastructure on women's employment in India. *Feminist Economics, 25*(4), 94–125.

Mammen, K., & Paxson, C. (2000). Women's work and economic development. *Journal of Economic Perspectives, 14*(4), 141–164.

Mbembé, J. A., & Nuttall, S. (2004). Writing the world from an African metropolis. *Public Culture, 16*(3), 347–372.

McFarlane, C. (2011). *Learning the city: Knowledge and translocal assemblage.* Wiley Blackwell.

Núñez, A., Benwell, M. C., & Aliste, E. (2022). Interrogating green discourses in Patagonia-Aysén (Chile): Green grabbing and eco-extractivism as a new strategy of capitalism? *Geographical Review, 112*(5), 688–706.

Onaran, Ö., Oyvat, C., & Fotopoulou, E. (2022). A macroeconomic analysis of the effects of gender inequality, wages, and public social infrastructure: The case of the UK. *Feminist Economics, 28*(2), 152–188.

Osunmuyiwa, O. O., & Ahlborg, H. (2022). Stimulating competition, diversification, or re-enforcing entrepreneurial barriers? Exploring small-scale electricity systems and gender-inclusive entrepreneurship. *Energy Research & Social Science, 89*, 102566.

Pieterse, E. (2008). *City futures: Confronting the crisis of urban development*. Zed Press.

Rozenberg, J., & Fay, M. (Eds.). (2019). *Beyond the gap: How countries can afford the infrastructure they need while protecting the planet. Sustainable infrastructure series*. World Bank.

Saldívar, E. (2014). 'It's not race, it's culture': Untangling racial politics in Mexico. *Latin American and Caribbean ethnic studies, 9*(1), 89–108.

Samad, H. A., & Zhang, F. (2019). Electrification and women's empowerment: Evidence from rural India. *World Bank Policy Research Working Paper* (8796).

Sandoval-Reyes, J., Idrovo-Carlier, S., & Duque-Oliva, E. J. (2021). Remote work, work stress, and work–life during pandemic times: A Latin America situation. *International Journal of Environmental Research and Public Health, 18*(13), 7069.

Shen, M., & Zamani, E. D. (2024). Gender differences in remote work: A study on the boundary management tactics of women and men. *Information Technology and People*.

Simone, A. M. (2008). The politics of the possible: Making urban life in Phnom Penh. *Singapore Journal of Tropical Geography, 29*(2), 186–204.

Simone, A. M. (2011). No longer the subaltern: Refiguring cities of the global south. In T. Ednesor & M. Jayne (Eds.), *Urban theory beyond the west: A world of cities* (pp. 31–46). Routledge.

Small, S. F., & van der Meulen Rodgers, Y. (2023). The gendered effects of investing in physical and social infrastructure. *World Development, 171*, Article 106347.

Sultana, F. (2022). The unbearable heaviness of climate coloniality. *Political geography, 99*, 102638.

Thomas, A. A. (2021). An investigation of the impact of occupational stress on the mental health of remote working women IT professionals in urban Bangalore, India. *Journal of International Women's Studies, 22*(6), 139–149.

UN Women. (2018). *Turning promises into action: Gender equality in the 2030 agenda for sustainable development*.

UN Women. (2022). *Progress on the sustainable development goals: The gender snapshot 2022*.

UNICEF. (2021). *Hygiene*. 152 WHO, 2022. *Progress on household drinking water, sanitation and hygiene 2000–2022: Special focus on gender*. New York: United Nations Children's Fund & World Health Organization.

UNICEF & WHO. (2022). *Progress on drinking water, sanitation and hygiene in Africa 2000–2020: Five years into the SDGs*. New York: United Nations Children's Fund (UNICEF) & World Health Organization.

World Bank. (2010). *Making infrastructure work for women and men: A review of World Bank infrastructure projects (1995–2009)*. Washington, DC: World Bank.

World Health Organization (WHO). (2017). *Safely managed drinking water: Thematic report on drinking water*. Geneva: World Health Organization.

World Health Organization (WHO). (2022). *World health statistics 2022: Monitoring health for the SDGs, sustainable development goals*. Geneva: World Health Organization.

Yanochik, M. A., Thornton, M., & Ewing, B. T. (2003). Railroad construction and antebellum slave prices. *Social Science Quarterly, 84*(3), 723–737.

Zacharia, L. (2014). *Factors causing gender inequality in education in Tanzania: A case of Korogwe District secondary schools*. Doctoral dissertation, The Open University of Tanzania.

Decolonising and Decarbonising the Economics Curriculum: An Exploration of Synergies

Alexandra Arntsen, Helen Puntha, and Melanie Gayana Welaratne

Abstract Current and future generations are facing multiple challenges in the form of climate change, ecological deterioration, and social inequalities. These interconnected issues are associated with costs which are only expected to increase over time. This has implications for higher education which needs to equip graduates with decarbonisation and decolonisation frameworks to tackle the complexities of the twenty-first century. This chapter pays attention to the way the economics curriculum can empower

A. Arntsen (✉)
Department of Economics, Nottingham Trent University, Nottingham, UK
e-mail: alexandra.arntsen@ntu.ac.uk

H. Puntha
School of Health and Medical Sciences, City St George's, University of London, London, UK
e-mail: hpuntha@sgul.ac.uk

M. G. Welaratne
Centre for Academic Development and Quality, Nottingham Trent University, Nottingham, UK
e-mail: melanie.welaratne@ntu.ac.uk

A. Agunsoye and A. Arntsen (eds.), *Decarbonising and Decolonising Economics*, https://doi.org/10.1007/978-3-032-11972-8_7

practitioners and learners to become changemakers capable of designing solutions for environmental and injustice crises.

Keywords Economics curriculum · Decolonisation · Decarbonisation · Education for sustainable development (ESD)

1 Introduction

The environmental impact of economic activity is well established in the literature,[1] illustrating how capitalist industrialisation, historically and presently, is driving environmental deterioration through exploitation of labour and the environment (Gill, 2024). The impacts of extractive economic activity, in the name of development, affect a broad range of groups as evidenced in recent climate disasters, but are disproportionately experienced by low income, indigenous, and future populations in terms of health, displacement, ecological destruction and losses of culture and community (Ambler, 2022). A growing related body of work is further highlighting how recent developments towards (inadequately defined) green capitalism is reinforcing these exploitative and extractive activities in ways that risk climate maladaptation. In other words, actions designed to help mitigate or adapt to climate change ultimately cause increased risk of harmful climate-related outcomes. This may be directly through increased greenhouse gas emissions, or indirectly by these actions exaggerating injustices, reducing welfare, creating an increased vulnerability to climate change or other environmental issues (Buller, 2022).

Extractivist economic activities tend to be undemocratic, even as governments and corporations justify them through financial transfers and growth motives. Jerez et al. (2021) exemplify this with how Latin American export-led extractivism is legitimised by strong state participation and a distribution of some of the surpluses in the form of social policies. This reinforces the colonial patterns with a monopolistic producer

[1] Such as increases in air pollution and extreme weather events, reductions in jobs and livelihoods, decreased water quality and food supply, increases in injuries, fatalities, malnutrition, illness, migration and conflict (SOS-UK, 2022) as well as poorer public health, lower life expectancy, and reduced longterm economic growth (Environment Agency, 2023).

and a dependence on demand from dominating economies. The move towards these unjust, extractivist economic activities is further intensified under the flag of the green transition. Dorn and Dietz (2024) exemplify how conflicts around land, livelihoods, and water have arisen due to Argentinian lithium extraction. The failure to address cultural and territorial rights in combination with the absence of participation rights in the process is resulting in involuntary resettlements, insufficient compensation and severe environmental destruction. This is occurring in combination with disputes over profit distribution, taxation, and the role of cultural representation in future development.

There is a risk that the notion of green activities will mean that issues such as those outlined above will be ignored in favour of legitimising narratives around climate protection, green development and industrialisation, and similar arguments under the umbrella of decarbonisation. The increasing demands of raw material essentials for transition to a decarbonised economy likewise risk repeating the same patterns of colonial extraction in a new format. It is crucial that economics, and other disciplines, develop the analytical tools needed to avoid reinforcing historical patterns of coloniality in the name of green development for decarbonisation.

Currently, the economic discipline and its curriculum tend to engage with decarbonisation in ways which pay little regard to broader sustainability concerns, including impacts on the economies producing materials essential for the transition (Arntsen, 2025). This is a barrier towards sustainable development, as education is key to empower individuals and communities with the knowledge and skills that enable them to develop values, attitudes, and behaviours that support sustainable change.

Economics is influential as it not only observes and analyses the world, but actively shapes it through assumptions, scope and norms (Graupe, 2012). It is therefore vital that education empowers economists to become decolonising scholars who challenge dispossession, oppression, and domination (D-Econ, n.d) while simultaneously work towards addressing climate change and broader environmental challenges. Students are key actors in this process, and their voices have been amongst the first to raise the need for decolonising and decarbonising education (SOS-UK, 2022). This chapter constitutes an invitation for dialogue around how we can create economics education wherein our students are empowered to create sustainable change through a decolonial lens.

To empower students, reinvigorate the economics discipline and contribute towards a climate-just transition, economics education needs to explore decarbonisation in ways which avoid reproducing unsustainable economic systems and instead incorporate decolonial and climate justice perspectives which prompt analysis with special attention to marginalised groups. This involves recognising that low-income and marginalised communities, with low historical contribution to global warming, are disproportionately impacted by climate change and ecological destruction. To reduce exploitation, oppression, and marginalisation, we must identify how the impact of climate change is experienced unevenly and in differentiated ways across different groups of people. A consequence of not acknowledging injustices is the systematic exclusion or marginalisation of groups which can be seen in the current climate change processes with the result that mitigation and adaptation interventions often reinforce issues around *how*, *where* and *why* different groups benefit from and lose out of the interventions (Sultana, 2022).

The chapter does not pertain to determine the only way forward but is intended to provide reflection points and inspiration for economics educators in relation to intersections of decolonisation and decarbonisation. This is enabled through an overview of the connections between decolonisation and decarbonisation and the economics curriculum, condensed into a set of reflective prompts for developing conscious practice.

The next section discusses broad insights from the literature on decolonising the curriculum and more specifically within economics. The subsequent part presents an overview of decarbonisation in a curriculum context, including the case of the economics discipline. This is followed by a discussion on key intersections between decolonisation and decarbonisation in the curriculum including a set of reflective questions. The chapter concludes with thoughts on moving forward.

2 Decolonising the Curriculum

In higher education, a curriculum is commonly referred to as the overall structure and content of a programme of study or a specific course. It outlines what students are expected to learn, how they will learn it and how their learning will be evaluated. It also establishes the guidelines for what the course team are expected to teach and how. In this chapter, we take a holistic view of curriculum. Alongside content and knowledge, we also consider the learning objectives, teaching methods, assessment strategies, opportunities to engage in research, practical experience, internships, and other forms of experience learning related to the field of study (Smith, 2000).

Universities are often seen as the centre for knowledge recognition, legitimisation, production, and reproduction. The epistemic structures of universities play a part in sustaining modern colonial world systems, disseminating Eurocentric knowledge as universal (Mignolo, 2011), thus creating a perpetuating cycle of reproducing colonial modes of thinking. Mbembe (2015) states that we must challenge the underlying assumption of a Eurocentric worldview in knowledge production. Eurocentrism has created a system where the only accepted knowledge is that produced by a limited group of scholars, trained in a limited set of methods, and stated to produce universal knowledge that can be applied to all—while disregarding the thinking and knowledge of all. This limits the empowerment and freedom of learning that could enable progressive, sustainable change.

The call to decolonise knowledge should "remind us that education should not be passive dissemination of 'knowledge'" (Belluigi, 2023: 138), and that as educators, we must take an active role in changing this viewpoint. When looking to decolonising the curriculum, we must critically reflect on what we as curators and stewards of the curriculum have chosen to include and why. Paulo Freire's (1970) work highlights that the oppressive systems within education go much deeper than the content and subjects we teach, and that disadvantages are deeply rooted in an epistemological and pedagogical level. Decolonising the curriculum is a continuous process of challenging and transforming the Eurocentric biases and colonial legacies present in educational context, structures, and practices. This requires educators to reflect on the core fundamentals of their disciplines and then rethink and develop these so that they incorporate a diverse range of voices (Smith, 2021).

As the foundations for each subject are different, it is also important for educators to develop approaches to decolonise curriculum which are sensitive to the specificities of the subject and relevant industries. De Lissovoy (2010) argues that decoloniality in higher education institutions requires a critical interrogation of the enduring legacies of colonialism in the production of knowledge and educational structures. This involves examining the values, rationalities, and epistemologies that shape our ways of knowing and being, as well as their connections to broader societal systems. This examination can highlight different challenges depending on the subject. Furthermore, we must recognise and value indigenous knowledge systems and relate these to the broader need for advancing economic and political justice through reparations.

Indigenous knowledge is often derived from experiences, experiments, creativity and innovation, held and transferred within local communities though oral history and shared activities. Decolonial approaches emphasise centring of these voices and worldviews in knowledge making (Masenya, 2022), which then informs the taught curriculum. This highlights that the impact and importance of decolonising the curriculum extend beyond the classroom, playing a crucial role in addressing broader socioeconomic historical injustices and global power dynamics.

2.1 Decolonising the Economics Curriculum

Decolonisation scholarship has a rich history, and recent movements such as Black Lives Matters have broadened engagement. This has allowed it to appear in the forefront of rethinking academic delivery by inspiring and shining attention to debates on forms and legacies of colonialism. From a disciplinary perspective, it has reinvigorated scrutiny of the inadequacies of economics in analysing structural and intersectional inequalities. Scholars such as Amin (1989) have explored how the discipline of economics has been shaped by Eurocentrism, using Western European industrialisation as the definition of development. This view of development extends beyond merely what is considered economic development to also acting as a framework for what is considered knowledge. A narrow worldview has limited what is thought of as recognised and rigorous academic thought, placing concepts such as rationality, objectivity, and profitability at the heart of the economics discipline. The reference point with a capitalist framework at the centre ascribes any non-European approaches, knowledge, and worldviews to otherness[2] (Charusheela & Zein-Elabdin, 2003). This is underlined by economics having a history of universalising its theorising in its pursuit to be a science. In addition to ignoring the fact that there are a multitude of ways to write economic theory, this endeavour allows treatment of other more complex

[2] Interrogation of Eurocentrism and otherness can with benefits be extended with Said's (1979) seminal work on orientalism and Zein-Elabdin's (2011) analysis of developmentalism.

theories as limited incidents with less explanatory power. Sidelining of "incomprehensible otherness" erases alternative explanations of economic development. This neglect creates a system that will compare all non-Western processes to the centre model and then consider them flawed (Kaul, 2003: 231).

Decolonising economics must involve radical evaluation and rethinking of the discipline, including theory, method, and analysis (Carrasco-Miró, 2025; Kvangraven & Kesar, 2023). Providing historical context, accepting and valuing concepts from outside the Global North, and acknowledging the contributions of previously ignored scholars are all part of this. It must enable critical confrontation of the current oppressions and dispossessions which extractivist capitalist systems encourage (Gopal, 2021).

Economics is sold as a science which observes, rather than as a social field where economists' own assumptions inform and shape reality. For example, economics education and introductory textbooks tend to unquestioningly accept an unequal distribution of wealth as an analytical starting point (Graupe, 2012). Ambler et al. (2022) explain how what is considered as credible knowledge directly influences the shape of the economy. If we *know* that there is an optimal level of pollution, then we can proceed to treat countries as under-polluted. Our assumptions shape the solutions we develop. This allows for a discipline which systematically reinforces injustices and extraction. Furthermore, studies have found that students' own values change to align with their field of study. The guise of neutrality in neoclassical economics allows for ignoring the values that underpin the school of thought, while developing graduate values in line with homo economicus, e.g. maximisation and rationality measured in hedonistic or monetary terms (Racko, 2019). This contradicts the aim of graduates who "think critically about the limits of their analysis in a broader socioeconomic context" and that have "critical and creative capacities beyond the application of existing tools and models" (QAA, 2023, pp. 4–6). The prevailing narrative within the economics discipline, and the dominant methods of teaching it in higher education, tend to reinforce a narrow set of neoliberal values. To evolve into a discipline that genuinely fosters a just transition, economics must challenge the logic shaped by these values. Spotton Visano (2016) emphasises the need for alternative worldviews and a pluralistic curriculum to equip students to think critically and exercise independent judgement in their future roles.

There is also a need for diversity of theoretical and methodological approaches, representation, and what is considered as knowledge, and this needs to be done on a structural level, rather than at the individual level where it is currently addressed. Diversification in representation, for example, is often treated on a one-to-one basis wherein the minority candidate is supported to fit into the expected role. This does not solve the issue of a non-diverse discipline, it simply moulds people into a set structure (Ambler et al., 2022). Although having a more diverse scholarship would be beneficial, diversity alone will not challenge the structural issues of the discipline (Shringarpure, 2020).

Consequently, decolonising economics means interrogating what is considered as core economic theory and method, and questioning who, how, and why these norms were established. While the Global North dominates the recognised knowledge production, many economic theories have been developed in global processes (McClure, 2021), and yet are not acknowledged accordingly (Gopal, 2021). For example, historical processes of colonisation and imperialism have created a biased and hierarchal view of what is seen as knowledge and who produces knowledge. The network Diversifying and Decolonising Economics (D-Econ) stresses the importance of (i) recognising the presence and role of Eurocentrism in economics; (ii) identifying and removing the barriers that exclude academics and thoughts outside those of the Global North, (iii) highlighting and confronting the discipline's claims of neutrality, and universality, (iv) and creating a field that enables the endeavour associated with decolonisation.

Economics claims to be a discipline equipped to explore any topic; however, it fails to acknowledge that it does so based on narrow methods. Economics focusses largely on quantitative analysis, with strong emphasis on modelling, and a belief of universality in approaches, rather than recognising local histories. Academia, and high-ranking journals often act as gatekeepers, controlling what kind of research methods are accepted (Choat et al., 2024). This narrow, technical approach is concentrated further in an educational setting, where there is less space for disagreements and confusion (Graupe, 2012). Students, and the practitioners they become, work from the theory and models they have learnt, often without knowing why these have been established as the mainstream paradigm. One step towards addressing this is introducing students to the pluralist reality of the economics discipline and raising their awareness of the diverse set of decolonial and postcolonial theories (including critiques within and of the practices). This can enable engagement with these theories and allow students to explore how a decolonial lens can reveal colonial patterns within the concepts and institutions that form the basis of economies (D-Econ, n.d).

The next section will turn our focus to decarbonisation of the curriculum. As with the process of decolonisation, the decarbonisation of the curriculum requires interrogation and renewal of disciplines; their theories, methods, analyses and how these are taught.

3 Decarbonising the Curriculum

Carbon concentration is a major driver of climate change, categorised by Richardson et al. (2023) as one of nine planetary boundaries essential for sustaining humanity. Seven of these boundaries, including climate change, have been breached by human activities, pushing us beyond sustainable margins. All planetary boundaries must be considered systemically, and this inseparability has implications for the effective design of decarbonisation strategies including those relating to the curriculum. Decarbonisation refers to reducing or removing carbon dioxide and other greenhouse gas (GHG) emissions from the earth's atmosphere and is recognised as a possible way of halting or reversing the human-driven climate and ecological emergency (Claeys et al., 2024).

In the UK, most universities have committed to decarbonising their Estates and Operations with strategies and related objectives, many of which include net-zero targets set earlier than national targets (Universities UK, 2024). In contrast, university strategy around education and research tends to be less explicitly linked to net-zero targets. Research activity in many universities does however contribute to decarbonisation, for example by deepening understanding of climate change and through development of sustainable materials and technologies. This research knowledge sometimes feeds into curriculum if researchers also teach students. The negative impacts of travel and large events related to research activity should, however, be acknowledged here. At the time of writing the authors are not aware of any UK university with an explicit decarbonisation strategy relating to their educational offer. Many students are only exploring decarbonisation within optional curriculum or extra-curricular offers. Where universities offer such extra-curricular training, it is rare that discussion of climate change and decarbonisation is connected back to the academic discipline. This can amplify the false notion that sustainability broadly and decarbonisation specifically bear little connection to the academic disciplines or related industries. There are exceptions to this where universities have incorporated subject-based climate education linked to industry including within core curriculum (see for example Molthan-Hill et al., 2017).

As our collective understanding of sustainability and its relationship to specific disciplines and industries becomes more nuanced it becomes apparent that to ensure adequate levels of sustainability literacy, sustainability must be mainstreamed into all disciplines through a subject-based approach (Gills & Morgan, 2021). Generic sustainability awareness education is no longer adequate to equip graduates with the knowledge, skills, and competencies needed to compete in the graduate job market, nor to contribute to the broadest sense as a citizen. Decarbonisation is most effectively incorporated within a disciplinary context to allow for depth and breadth of exploration. It is a multi-faceted and complex issue with ramifications for economies and societies as well as the environment. In this way it lends itself to both disciplinary and interdisciplinary examination. Decarbonisation education currently lacks maturity (Vogel et al, 2023) but has the potential to be a tool to transform content and delivery of teaching and learning, ensuring that students have the competencies needed to address and overcome the climate crisis (SOS-UK, 2022).

3.1 Decarbonising the Economics Curriculum

Economics as a discipline has largely failed to fully address climate change and ecological degradation (Pirgmaier, 2017; Racko, 2019; Røpke, 2020). Schor (2010) argues that the weak treatment of the environment in mainstream neoclassical economic analysis may be a key reason why economics has failed to pick up on the ecological disaster we are facing today. The field of climate economics has received broad criticism for methodological misconceptions which have contributed to delays and policy inaction, worsening the climate crisis. For example, work by Nobel Prize winner Nordhaus (2018) has claimed that global warming will have a limited effect on global GDP.[3] These low estimates of climate change impact enable governments and organisations to give a lower priority to what climate researchers show is an urgent and catastrophic outcome (Keen, 2021).

[3] Estimating that a 3 °C global warming would cause a 2.1% reduction in global GDP compared to the growth without any climate change. It proceeds to suggest that larger changes such as 6 °C increase in global warming would merely reduce GDP by 8.5%.

Criticism of economics education argues that the core subjects do not tend to acknowledge interactions between the economy and the environment (Common & Stagl, 2005; Gills & Morgan, 2021). The discipline has made progress by incorporating features such as carbon pricing, ascribing property rights and market prices to pollution, and, by extension, partially determining prices of the quality of certain natural resources. However, these notions are still treated as add-ons, addressed within a segment of a module, rather than framed as essential parts of the economics curriculum. This means that learners can become economists with very little insight into the role of the environment and natural resources within economies. Many environmental resources which lack property rights and prices are treated as externalities and are therefore considered secondary goods within the mainstream approach. Although it can be argued that carbon pricing ascribes property rights and market prices to pollution, which by extension sets a price of the quality of air/water, warnings highlight that only a limited amount of emissions are priced and prices are inadequate with regards to damages (Claeys et al., 2024). Models treating environmental/ecological values as fundamental variables have moved away from core macroeconomic and microeconomic analysis to sub-disciplines. This occurrence has enabled economists to carry on with theories and models which behave as if ecological values do not exist (Common & Stagl, 2005). This has a knock-on effect as numerous disciplines routinely draw upon mainstream economic theory to illuminate phenomenon studied within their own domains (such as sociology, psychology, politics, and maths), making them vulnerable to the same methodological misconceptions around climate economics. This has implications for how climate knowledge is taught, researched, and applied across a variety of spheres (Stratford, 2024). In this way, the delay to addressing decarbonisation within mainstream economics is holding back decarbonisation education within other disciplines.

Students are usually taught that economic agents are driven by hedonistic maximisation, measured in monetary terms such as output, profit, and consumption levels. Although they may briefly read work from Easterlin (2021) and many others on the paradox of the disappearing income and happiness correlation after meeting basic needs, this is rarely developed to incorporate how higher levels of consumption directly reduce wellbeing by destroying life-supporting ecosystems. The environmental omission has been raised by both students and academics, especially in heterodox approaches, where environmental and ecological issues are increasingly featured (Røpke, 2020). The increasing urgency of the climate issue has created broad calls for mainstreaming Education for Sustainable Development (ESD) into all levels of education.

The recently revised Economics Subject Benchmark Statement now specifies that Economic graduates need to have skills which enable them to manage and create solutions for the planetary crisis (QAA, 2023). The UN-supported initiative Principles for Responsible Management Education aims to integrate ESD into economics education by increasing the sustainability focus within business schools, equipping students to create change in line with the Sustainable Development Goals (SDGs). Relevant critique of SDGs highlights their focus on micro-level goals based on the commodification of people as labour, nature as land, and exchange as money, rather than on how to permanently increase global living standards (Arora-Jonsson, 2023). This shifts attention to symptoms such as individual countries' deficiencies, rather than exploring and tackling underlying causes such as global power relations which ultimately defend the prevalence of extractive systems, institutions, and economic projects. Without careful design, treatment of the SDGs including decarbonisation within economics (and other) curriculum can therefore perpetuate coloniality (Olstead & Chattopadhyay, 2023).

An area that currently largely evades the mainstream economic curriculum is the growth debate. The assumption that increased quantities bring greater satisfaction is posed in the first year of study, never to be questioned or even acknowledged as a mere postulation (Graupe, 2012). The mainstream economics curriculum rarely questions whether growth in itself should be a goal. This is despite an increasing problematisation of the growth hegemony and a growing call for degrowth within academic literature and a wider social movement. Degrowth, as defined by Spash and Asara (2018), is a democratic approach to reducing production and consumption, while diminishing the central role of markets in organising human life; aimed at achieving environmental sustainability, social justice, and well-being. It rejects the idea of green growth, highlighting that whilst such efforts as renewable energy advancements may achieve relative decoupling of economic activity from resource use, it cannot achieve absolute decoupling. A key criticism is the difficulty to accurately measure decoupling given the interrelationships of ecological phenomenon. Add to this the fact that decarbonisation, to meet the Paris Agreement target of 1.5 or 2 °C, requires absolute decoupling,[4] that means a fall in emissions irrespective of growth on a global level. Current trends in decreasing national emissions are exaggerated by measuring carbon based on production rather than consumption, effectively relocating recorded emissions to net-exporting countries (Tallgauer & Schank, 2024) with no evidence of global decoupling (Claeys et al., 2024).

Degrowth stresses that the growth focus within economics is not only ecologically unsustainable but also poses issues for equity and justness, raising questions around an assumed positive relationship between economic activity and wellbeing (Lang, 2024). Scholars, such as Røpke (2020) and Tallgauer and Schank (2024), thus call for a recentring of economics education around provisioning, focussing on improving living standards and thriving. Like the decolonisation movement, proponents argue for plurality and transdisciplinarity, highlighting the inherent normativity of economics and that economic theory and policy is not neutral or apolitical but underpinned by specific values, world views, and assumptions. In addition, their guiding principles include collaboration, social development, and agency to develop learners who can create sustainable change towards a prosperous society. Their suggestion for rethinking the economics curriculum includes historic and contemporary accounts of equity and access to resources, for example in relation to colonial extraction, the influence of the World Bank and current debates on climate finance. This chapter extends that further, by discussing how decoloniality adds key understandings for making economics education more sustainable. As the challenges open up new ways of thinking, it is an interesting time to explore how to decarbonise and decolonise the economic discipline.

4 Intersections of Decolonisation and Decarbonisation

Economic activity is, historically to the present day, linked with colonial exploitation and carbon emissions. The fossil fuel industry has contributed to the dispossession and destruction of communities, land, and ecological

[4] It should be noted that decoupling is a debated concept, see for example Warlenius (2025).

systems in addition to driving climate change (Ambler, 2022). A movement away from fossil fuel utilisation is therefore seen as a positive and just transition. However, numerous scholars (Lang et al., 2024, Ramirez et al., 2024) have raised concerns that the greening of economic activities risks extending the historical relationship between economic activities and colonialism, disguised under the promise of climate solutions.

Sultana (2023: paragraph 6) introduces the term "climate coloniality", a reference to the numerous ways patterns of colonialism are echoed in the climate issue. Colonial and imperial legacies of exploitation and structural racism shape power over climate policies, solutions, and financing as well as distribution of impact. Sultana explains how this stems from the uneven distribution of the human-made climate crisis "driven by the relentless pursuit of capitalist profit and power" (paragraph 4). This imbalance has its legacy in colonial and imperial systems which shape who has the power to set out climate policy, interventions and how this should be financed, as well as the circumstances which have led to the climate vulnerable communities we see today. The most vulnerable groups, with little historic contribution to the exploitation and ignorance of environmental values, carry the largest climate impacts. At the same time, the power to shape climate change responses and policy is largely controlled by a smaller number of leading states and corporations. The role of coloniality in climate governance has been called out by activists, stressing issues such as equity and justice. Coolsaet et al. (2024) extends the argument by explaining how indigenous and racialised communities tend to have less access to environmental and climate processes in combination with a sidelining of their needs, knowledge, and values.

Sultana (2023) stresses how students need tools to explore patterns of power dynamics, inequities and injustices through "voices, experiences and knowledge systems of diverse Black, Indigenous and people of colour in climate solutions, while also learning from communities in the Global South" (paragraph 10). Economics discourse must address structural exclusion and recognise indigenous sovereignty and freedom (Carrasco-Miró, 2025). This is of high importance in the economic discipline where students need to be exposed to value systems that do not encourage the pursuit of self-interest of sub-groups such as shareholders over wider stakeholders, or that deem ethical goals and wellbeing "irrational" (Racko, 2019: 38). Decarbonising education without adopting a decolonial lens risks reinforcing and intensifying colonial patterns.

The centrality of a capitalist economy as the standard, and the focus on economic growth as a main economic objective, has moved economics further from sustainable development. Growth is a core feature of capitalism, assumed as a requirement for progress and development and has become central to understanding the economy (Schmelzer et al., 2022). The growth hegemony has been problematised in terms of its ecological and social impacts. A key environmental concern is the path dependence between economic growth and GHG emissions, as economic activity is locked-in to extraction and burning of non-renewable energy fuels on multiple levels, and over interdependent systems (Bulkeley et al., 2022). There are critiques to growth's ability to solve social issues such as inequality. While capitalist ideology argues that economic growth will naturally "trickle down" to all levels of society (Ndhlovu, 2019: 74), empirical literature reveals an absence of a straightforward relationship between GDP growth and poverty reduction. Furthermore, "most economic growth in the Global South is achieved through economic activities which have a negative impact on well-being", causing further disparities (Lang, 2024, p. 923).

5 Starting a Decolonised and Decarbonised Practice

This section presents an exploration of key synergies between the need for decolonisation and decarbonisation of the economics curriculum. The authors' different perspectives due to their varying roles in higher education as well as individual positionalities, have been united in an exploration of steps towards developing a decolonised and decarbonised economics curriculum. The literature has highlighted how decolonising the curriculum necessitates thinking critically about power, knowledge structures, and approaches. Progressive scholarly work provides evidence of ambitious efforts on how economics can be reformed by interrogating our practice (Choat et al., 2024; Kvangraven & Kesar, 2023; Pirgmaier, 2017; Røpke, 2020; Tallgauer & Schank, 2024).

Agunsoye et al. (2022) encapsulate how we can produce a more just future discipline and curriculum through a set of reflective questions which we summarise as:

1. Who are we teaching, what is taught, and by whom?

2. How do we teach and assess, and in what way is teaching influenced by research?
3. What specific challenges and opportunities do we face with regards to diversifying, decolonising and democratising academic economics?

We argue, in line with growing movements, that decarbonisation (and wider ESD) is more powerful when considered in combination with a decolonial interrogation. We suggest four areas with prompts for reflection to identify and stimulate opportunities to apply decolonisation and decarbonisation in the economics curriculum. We envisage that these prompts will be used by educators who are looking to develop their curriculum.

1. *What are the main assumptions within introductory economic subjects? How were these established? What implications do these have for climate justice,and where does your teaching present alternative theoretical viewpoints which interrogate these aspects?*

   These prompts aim to encourage an interrogation of the mainstream economic assumptions introduced as principles of the discipline. Consider the assumptions of homo economicus, the rational consumer who is always trying to maximise utility. We need to question mainstream economics' hedonistic focus on utility, measured in quantitative terms, illustrated in increasing indifference curves, and interpreted as higher levels of consumption. This neoclassical approach of inherent economic behaviour translates to a growth lock-in in consecutive analyses. This is despite the misfit between homo economicus and real individuals' economic behaviour; an inconsistency whose effects include significant sustainability consequences.

   We need to start examining the growth hegemony which is often established already in students' first encounter with economics. This includes the worldview(s) that these assumptions entail at the introductory stages of education, and to what degree this reduces economics to a monoculture or a more pluralist subject. A key criticism of introductory economics education is that learners are not made aware that mainstream economics is an approach, rather, students are made to believe that they simply study *economics*.

It would therefore be valuable for academics and practitioners to consider how they have aligned with the mainstream approach, recognising that this delivery is attached to a certain worldview. It could be beneficial to consider the level of pluralism in our economics curriculum, which can explore the diversity of theoretical perspectives as well as methodological pluralism.

2. *How does your teaching introduce the allocation problem around what to produce, how to produce, and how much of it?*

   This prompt can be expanded to consider if and how our teaching develops the concept of sustainable production further than efficiency, considering aspects such as resource origin, use and waste management throughout the supply-chain. This reflection needs to be contextualised within global justice, resource limitations, distribution, and to consider desired scale of the economy. The aim is to question the initial distribution of resources and structural inequalities in our economy. The current approach argues that economic growth will increase wellbeing for everyone, but even if we ignore evidence disproving this theory, it is clear that ever-increasing quantity has direct consequences for sustainability. The debate can be extended to how efficiency is defined, for whom it is efficient and how it will be achieved. An important area to consider with regard to sustainable production is resource use. Who is producing resources and who is consuming them? How are the benefits of this production distributed? A broader discussion is the nature of sustainable production—can we expect positive, linear growth in a world of finite resources?

3. *How does your course discuss relationships between economic activity, carbon dioxide, and broader environmental degradation? Additionally, how does it incorporate reflections on how structural and colonial patterns contribute to these persistent issues?*

   These questions aim to highlight the direct links between economic activity and environmental degradation, paying attention to the role of capitalist worldviews. This discussion needs to be framed within an understanding of different aspects of the relationships, such as timeframe (whether links are historic or present-day), geographical scope (regional, national, or global), choice of data measurements (for example whether carbon measurements are based on origin of production or consumption) and pollutants (all GHG emissions and other pollutants such as nitrogen dioxide). This analysis can be developed by examining how colonialism is associated with exploitation of land, labour and resources. Colonialism has created the basis for a range of environmental challenges that are experienced now, established in global patterns of exploitation and resource extraction in the economic–environment relationship.

4. *How does your teaching explore the role of institutions? Which institutions are considered, how are these identified,and what value judgements have informed this process?*

   These questions aim to enable reflection on how institutions are shaped over time and are subject to change, rather than as exogenous to the analysis. To understand current institutions through their historical context, students need an outline of the history and development of capitalism. While the economic discipline currently teaches the role of institutions, some even introducing the field of institutional economics, the material used tends to be selectively exclusive of certain institutions, failing to explore for example the role of slavery as an institution. Are students who are not exposed to critiques of economic theory in relation to societal institutions at risk of legitimising the viewpoint of European institutions, or even the imperial and colonial processes that established these, as supreme?

Openly acknowledging the limitations of claims that economics analyses the world through objective lens and without value judgments, can create space for learners to challenge the ways in which economic processes, such as globalisation, have been shaped by a Eurocentric worldview with neoclassic individual optimisation. This then allows learners to explore who is favoured by certain laws, who created these laws, with which expertise, and who upholds these laws. Likewise, questions can be raised about the role of democracy in economics and the value of centring the needs and values of communities most affected at the heart of goals and policies. As a result, students become able to engage with a pluralism of theories and methods, including an analysis of history, oppression, and power as starting points to understanding how economies are created and operate. These issues can be considered further using intersectional analysis and systems thinking, developing key competencies in students.

6 Conclusion

This chapter has discussed the need to decolonise the curriculum as a vital move towards addressing the intellectual, cultural, environmental and social damage done by colonialism. An overview of the literature on decolonisation suggests that despite ongoing efforts to decolonise social sciences, economics remains a less penetrable discipline (Kayatekin, 2009). Recent movements such as Rethinking Economics and D-Econ stress that economics is of particular importance due to its relationship to race and Eurocentrism (Alves & Kvangraven, 2021). This, in combination with economists' role as not just analysing but shaping the field of economics, highlights the need for an economics education which enables and empowers students to use a decolonial lens in their practice. As educators we do not need to come up with solutions in isolation. Instead, we can engage students as active creators in the decolonisation process. Simultaneously, we face challenges associated with climate change. Addressing the imminent threat requires decarbonisation efforts towards net-zero emissions on a global level. To undertake and achieve this enormous task there is a need to mainstream decarbonisation and ESD into all levels of society. There is particular interest in ensuring attention is paid to decarbonisation and sustainability more generally within education, to empower and enable future graduates to become agents of social change (Tallgauer & Schank, 2024). This is of major importance in economics, as there is a direct link between economic activity and ecological impact, driven by burning of fossil fuels, resource use, and exploitative extractivism.

This chapter has highlighted how these two challenges are inherently interlinked, and that a successful decarbonisation curriculum requires decolonisation in order to enable students to challenge practice and work towards climate justice. A curricular transformation towards mainstreaming of sustainability must be interlinked with a decolonisation of the curriculum in an ongoing process of developing the discipline (Ambler et al., 2022). While a challenging, and at times difficult, process we argue that introducing learners to dilemmas which governments and others are facing is enhancing graduate employability.

Finally, this chapter has presented a set of questions to help start the process of considering decolonisation and decarbonisation in the economics curriculum. The aim of these is to enable reflection on how current practice can be reimagined to facilitate open, respectful and rigorous discussion about the challenges that we face today, and the opportunities and options available to address these. As stressed by Sabaratnam (2017), this requires a university for all students, cultivating skills such as critical reasoning, courage and openness.

It is important to say that this chapter and the prompts are not an end-all guideline of decolonisation and decarbonisation, but rather a discussion we hope to see developed further in collaboration with colleagues and learners. This chapter aims to expand and connect the debates, leading to more responsive and responsible economic citizenship. As the chapter is not exhaustive, we acknowledge the need for decolonisation and decarbonisation in a wider setting, which could be investigated by further research.

References

Agunsoye, A., Groenewald, M., Guizzo, D., & Ramburuth-Hurt, K. (2022). Reforming academia. In L. Ambler, J. Earle, N. Scott, & J. Froud (Eds.), *Reclaiming economics for future generations.* Manchester: Manchester University Press.

Alves, C., & Kvangraven, I. H. (2021). *#Economicsfest: does economics need to be 'decolonised'*? https://www.economicsobservatory.com/economicsfest-does-economics-need-to-be-decolonised#:~:text=Decolonising%20the%20subject%2C%20from%20her%20perspective%2C%20is%20about,economics%20to%20be%20a%20discipline%20with%20universal%20laws. Accessed 13 June 2025.

Ambler, L., Earle, J., Scott, N., & Froud, J. (2022). *Reclaiming economics for future generations*. Manchester University Press.

Amin, S. (1989). *Eurocentrism.* NYU Press.

Arntsen, A. (2025). Climate justice, decolonisation, decarbonisation, and economics. In L. Chester & A. Bernasek (Eds.), *The Edward Elgar handbook of women and heterodox economics: Past, present, and future*. Edward Elgar Publishing.

Arora-Jonsson, S. (2023). The sustainable development goals: A universalist promise for the future. *Futures, 146*, 1.

Belluigi, D. Z. (2023). Why decolonising "knowledge" matters: Deliberations for educators on that made fragile. In P. Gibbs (Ed.), *Higher education for good: Teaching and learning futures.* Open Book Publishers.

Bulkeley, H., Stripple, J., Nilsson, L. J., van Veelen, B., Kalfagianni, A., Bauer, F., & van Sluisveld, M. (2022). *Decarbonising economies*. Cambridge University Press.

Buller, A. (2022). *The value of a whale: On the illusions of green capitalism*. Manchester University Press.

Carrasco-Miró, G. (2025). *Decolonizing feminist economics: Possibilities for just futures*. Bristol University Press.

Charusheela, S., & Zein-Elabdin, E. (2003). *Postcolonialism meets economics*. Taylor & Francis Group.

Choat, S., Wolf, C., & O'Neill, S. (2024). Decolonising economics and politics curricula in UK universities. *Studies in Higher Education, 49*(9), 1504–1518.

Claeys, G., LeMouel, M., Tagliapietra, S., Wolff, G. B., & Zachmann, G. (2024). *The Macroeconomics of decarbonisation: Implications and policies*. Cambridge University Press.

Common, M. S., & Stagl, S. (2005). *Ecological economics : An introduction*. Cambridge University Press.

Coolsaet, B., Agyeman, J., Kashwan, P., Rivera, D. Z., Ryder, S., Schlosberg, D., & Sultana, F. (2024). Acknowledging the historic presence of justice in climate research. *Nature Climate Change, 15*(2), 121.

De Lissovoy, N. (2010). Decolonial pedagogy and the ethics of the global. *Discourse: Studies in the Cultural Politics of Education, 31*(3), 279–293.

D-Econ (n.d) Our Mission. https://d-econ.org/mission/. Accessed 14 June 2024.

Dorn, F. M., & Dietz, K. (2024). Legitimising lithium mining: Global energy transition and green developmentalism in Jujuy, Argentina. *European Review of Latin American and Caribbean Studies, 118*, 43–66.

Easterlin, R. A. (2021). *An economist's lessons on happiness: Farewell dismal science*. Springer.

Environment Agency. (2023). *State of the environment: Health, people and the environment*. Environment Agency, London https://www.gov.uk/government/publications/state-of-the-environment/state-of-the-environment-health-people-and-the-environment (open in a new window). Accessed 22 May 2025.

Freire, P. (1970). *Pedagogy of the oppressed*. Seabury Press.

Gill, B. (2024). The political ecology of colonial capitalism: Race, nature, and accumulation. Manchester University Press.

Gills, B., & Morgan, J. (2021). Teaching climate complacency: Mainstream economics textbooks and the need for transformation in economics education. *Globalizations, 18*(7), 1189–1205.

Gopal, P. (2021). On decolonisation and the university. *Textual Practice, 35*(6), 873–899.

Graupe, S. (2012). The power of ideas. The teaching of economics and its image of man. *Journal of Social Science Education, 11*(2), 60–84.

Jerez, B., Garcés, I., & Torres, R. (2021). Lithium extractivism and water injustices in the Salar de Atacama, Chile: The colonial shadow of green electromobility. *Political Geography, 87*, Article 102382.

Kaul, N. (2003). Writing economic theory another way. In E. O. Zein-Elabdin & S. Charusheela (Eds.), *Postcolonialism meets economics*. Routledge.

Kayatekin, S. (2009). Between political economy and postcolonial theory: First encounters. *Cambridge Journal of Economics, 33*(6), 1113–1118.

Keen, S. (2021). The appallingly bad neoclassical economics of climate change. *Globalizations, 18*(7), 1149–1177.

Kvangraven, I. H., & Kesar, S. (2023). Standing in the way of rigor? Economics' meeting with the decolonization agenda. *Review of International Political Economy, 30*(5), 1723–1748.

Lang, M. (2024). Degrowth, global asymmetries, and ecosocial justice: Decolonial perspectives from Latin America. *Review of International Studies, 50*(5), 921–931.

Masenya, T. M. (2022). Decolonization of indigenous knowledge systems in South Africa: Impact of policy and protocols. *International Journal of Knowledge Management, 18*(1), 1–22.

Mbembe, A. (2015). *Decolonizing knowledge and the question of the archive*. Africa is a Country. https://wiser.wits.ac.za/system/files/Achille%20Mbembe%20-%20Decolonizing%20Knowledge%20and%20the%20Question%20of%20the%20Archive.pdf. Accessed 13 June 2025.

McClure, J. (2021). Connected global intellectual history and the decolonisation of the curriculum. *History Compass, 19*(1), 1.

Mignolo, W. D. (2011). *The darker side of western modernity: Global futures*. Duke University Press, Durham.

Molthan-Hill, P., Winfield, F., Baddley, J., & Hill, S. (2017). Work based learning: Students solving sustainability challenges through strategic business partnerships. In P. Flynn, M. Gudić, & T. Tan (Eds.), *Redefining success: integrating the UN global compact into management education. PRME*. Routledge.

Ndhlovu, T. P. (2019). Elusive solutions to poverty and inequality: From 'Trickle Down' to 'Solidarity Economy.' In S. J. Ndlovu-Gatsheni & B. Mpofu (Eds.), *Rethinking and unthinking development: Perspectives on inequality and poverty in South Africa and Zimbabwe*. Berghahn Books.

Nordhaus, W. (2018). Projections and uncertainties about climate change in an era of minimal climate policies. *American Economic Journal. Economic Policy, 10*(3), 333–360.

Olstead, R., & Chattopadhyay, S. (2023). Circles and lines: Indigenous ontologies and decolonising climate change education. *Settler Colonial Studies, 14*(1), 41–58.

Pirgmaier, E. (2017). The neoclassical Trojan horse of steady-state economics. *Ecological Economics, 133*, 52–61.

Quality Assurance Agency. (2023). *Subject benchmark statement: Economics*. https://web.archive.org/web/20230503152622/https://www.qaa.ac.uk/docs/qaa/sbs/sbs-economics-23.pdf?sfvrsn=e271a881_4. Accessed 12 June 2025.

Racko, G. (2019). The values of economics. *Journal of Business Ethics, 154*, 35–48.

Ramirez, J., Vélez-Zapata, C. P., & Maher, R. (2024). Green colonialism and decolonial feminism: A study of Wayúu women's resistance in La Guajira. *Human Relations, 77*(7), 937–964.

Richardson, K., Steffen, W., Lucht, W., Bendtsen, J., Cornell, S. E., Donges, J. F., Drüke, M., Fetzer, I., Bala, G., von Bloh, W., Feulner, G., Fiedler, S., Gerten, D., Gleeson, T., Hofmann, M., Huiskamp, W., Kummu, M., Mohan, C., Nogués-Bravo, D., ... Rockström, J. (2023). Earth beyond six of nine planetary boundaries. *Science Advances, 9*(37), 1.

Røpke, I. (2020). Econ 101—In need of a sustainability transition. *Ecological Economics, 169*, Article 106515.

Sabaratnam, M. (2017). *Decolonising intervention: International statebuilding in Mozambique*. Rowman & Littlefield.

Said, E. W. (1979). *Orientalism*. Vintage Books.

Schmelzer, M., Vetter, A., & Vansintjan, A. (2022). *The future is degrowth: A guide to a world beyond capitalism*. Verso Books.

Schor, J. (2010). *Plenitude: The new economics of true wealth*. Penguin Press.

Shringarpure, B. (2020). *Notes on fake decolonization*. https://africasacountry.com/2020/12/notes-on-fake-decolonization. Accessed 12 June 2025.

Smith, L. T. (2021). *Decolonizing methodologies: Research and indigenous peoples* (3rd ed.). Zed Books.

Smith, M. K. (2000). *Curriculum theory and practice*. The Encyclopedia of Pedagogy and Informal Education. http://infed.org/mobi/curriculum-theory-and-practice/. Accessed 12 June 2025.

SOS-UK. (2022). *New offering: Decolonising, decarbonising & democratising education workshop*. https://www.sos-uk.org/post/d3-workshop. Accessed 12 June 2025.

Spash, C. L., & Asara, V. (2018). Ecological economics. From nature to society. In L. Fischer (Ed.), *Rethinking economics: an introduction to pluralist economics*. Routledge.

Spotton Visano, B. (2016). Defying the dominant discourse: Why contesting neoliberalism needs critical pedagogy in economics education. *Critical Studies in Education, 60*(3), 321–339.

Stratford, R. J. (2024). Towards ecological everything—The ecological university, ecological subjectivity and the ecological curriculum. *Policy Futures in Education, 22*(7), 1338–1356.

Sultana, F. (2022). Critical climate justice. *The Geographical Journal, 188*(1), 118–124.

Sultana, F. (2023). *Fossil fuel exec is slated to lead COP28.* We must decolonize climate governance. https://truthout.org/articles/fossil-fuel-exec-is-slated-to-lead-cop28-we-must-decolonize-climate-governance/. Accessed 13 June 2025.

Tallgauer, M., & Schank, C. (2024). Challenging the growth-prosperity Nexus: Redefining undergraduate economics education for the Anthropocene. *Ecological Economics, 216*, Article 108026.

Universities UK. (2024). *Climate crisis: What progress have universities made*? https://www.universitiesuk.ac.uk/latest/insights-and-analysis/climate-crisis-what-progress-have. Accessed 12 February 2025.

Vogel, M., Parker, L., Porter, J., O'Hara, M., Tebbs, E., Gard, R., He, X., & Gallimore, J. B. (2023). *Education for sustainable development: A review of the literature.* AdvanceHE. https://www.advance-he.ac.uk/knowledge-hub/education-sustainable-development-review-literature-2015-2022. Accessed 12 June 2025.

Warlenius, R. H. (2025). Decoupling pessimism and the dilemma of growth. A reply to Jackson et al. (2024). *Ecological Economics, 232*, 108580.

Zein-Elabdin, E. (2011). Postcoloniality and development: Development as a colonial discourse. In L. Keita (Ed.), *Philosophy and African development: Theory and practice.* CODESRIA.

Conclusion

Ariane Agunsoye and Alexandra Arntsen

Abstract The concluding chapter brings together the central themes of the book by arguing that meaningful climate action must include transformative rethinking of economic systems, curricula, and policy frameworks to enable climate justice, reparations, and the creation of space for pluralistic worldviews. By highlighting the interconnectedness of colonial histories, ecological degradation, and global inequality, the authors call for a just transition that empowers communities, reconsiders the notion of development, and embeds sustainability within reimagined governance structures.

Keywords Inequalities · Climate action · Climate justice

A. Agunsoye (✉)
School of Creative Management, Goldsmiths, University of London, London, UK
e-mail: A.Agunsoye@gold.ac.uk

A. Arntsen
Department of Economics, Nottingham Trent University, Nottingham, UK
e-mail: alexandra.arntsen@ntu.ac.uk

A. Agunsoye and A. Arntsen (eds.), *Decarbonising and Decolonising Economics*, https://doi.org/10.1007/978-3-032-11972-8_8

This book has examined the intersecting challenges of decolonisation and decarbonisation in economics, questioning how Eurocentric paradigms constrain global climate action. By applying a decolonial lens to economic systems and climate initiatives, it explores how incorporating diverse worldviews can make the discipline more inclusive and better equipped to meet ecological demands of the twenty-first century. The impacts of climate change are deeply unequal (Sultana, 2022), and while decarbonisation is essential to limit warming to 1.5 °C and avoid irreversible damage (IPCC, 2023), current efforts remain insufficient. Yet the knowledge and tools to act decisively already exist. Achieving climate justice, however, will require decolonising the decarbonisation process.

The arguments presented in this book demonstrate how a mainstream economic approach is not just insufficient for addressing the sustainability challenges, but has actively contributed to them. Coloniality and economics are closely linked, historically and today. European imperial expansion consolidated economic dominance through violence and subjugation of land and people, fortified by a notion of cultural superiority. These patterns of coloniality were deepened with the industrial revolution and the intensification of capitalism. The emergence of capitalism as the dominant economic system, with Europe as the standard for thought, technology and institutions, established a narrow approach to development as the norm, casting capitalist growth as the rational and natural trajectory for all economies (Bhambra, 2023). A central argument running through the volume is that neoclassical economics, rather than being a neutral tool for understanding the world, has served as an active agent in reproducing these inequalities. By privileging efficiency, growth, and market rationality, it has obscured questions of justice, power, and ecological limits. Its models systematically externalise environmental costs, treating climate breakdown as a peripheral 'market failure' rather than an existential crisis, and in doing so have legitimised extractivist, carbon-intensive growth. In this sense, economics has not simply failed to resolve the climate crisis but has normalised and legitimised the very structures driving it. This complicity explains why mainstream approaches continue to favour carbon trading, technological fixes, and market-based solutions, even as these reproduce inequality and delay structural transformation. By foregrounding the role of economics in creating and sustaining climate injustice, the chapters collectively call for a profound rethinking of the discipline itself, not only in terms of curricular reform, but in its underlying epistemologies, its conception of growth, and its relationship to power.

As stressed by Lukka there is a need for reparative justice if decarbonisation is to integrate decolonial elements. Global wealth distribution, enabled by colonial extraction and resource depletion, has yet to be fully addressed, and the damage continues. Colonial extraction underpins both poverty and climate injustice. Addressing these historical and ongoing injustices necessitates a decarbonisation strategy that goes beyond pricing pollution, moving instead towards climate justice through decolonial approaches. Lukka further highlights that policies addressing redistribution and multinational corporations' tax evasion are crucial for confronting the legacies of economic coloniality and creating fiscal space for climate adaptation.

The failure of mainstream economics to account for climate costs and the resulting policy inaction has exacerbated the impacts of climate change. In contrast, progressive economic alternatives offer more insights into the ecological limits of the current economic system. 'The triplet crisis', as described by Chen and Bougiatiotis, underscores the need to address decolonisation and decarbonisation together in order to respond to the ecological emergency in a just manner. This requires moving beyond a Eurocentric worldview and centring the demands of the Global South, rather than treating these regions as passive participants in the transition to net zero. The net-zero transition must be just, grounded in democratic solutions, and involve a break from business-as-usual, along with reduced resource demands placed on the Global South by the Global North (Zografos, 2022). This book is an appeal for a more ambitious decolonisation transitioning towards climate justice, as showcased in the unique discussions provided here.

Following this discussion, Basin presents how dominant approaches, relying heavily on business as usual and technological fixes, worsen inequality, and environmental harm, while further concentrating power in a small number of countries and organisations. A just decarbonisation must instead support alternative movements that challenge the extractive, productivity-focused logic of mainstream economics. These movements should emphasise the political and social nature of ecological issues, requiring diverse, and decentralised solutions that empower Indigenous and local groups and incorporate their existing knowledge and practices.

Decarbonisation also entails a profound transformation in resource dependency, with minerals and metals playing a central role in the shift to renewable energy. Ghorbani, Nwaila, and Hugh Rose highlight how this transition is not merely technical or economic, but raises urgent questions around governance, equity, and sustainability. The increasing demand for critical minerals and materials risks reinforcing exploitative, colonial patterns of resource extraction in the Global South. A just net-zero transition requires moving beyond extractivist models towards decolonised approaches to resource governance. Decarbonisation must therefore be embedded within broader frameworks of justice, accountability, and inclusive decision-making.

Interrogating knowledge formation, what is considered or dismissed, is also key to decolonisation. Fotopoulou demonstrates how Eurocentric agendas dominate current definitions of infrastructure, shaping economic inclusion, access, and climate outcomes, which in turn distorts our understanding of development and reinforces inequality. Without a global definition, countries rely on inconsistent standards, directly affecting environmental goals, as infrastructure definitions are dominated by high-emission sectors such as energy, mining, and transport, with 'green' infrastructure not being clearly defined. Fotopoulou proposes a progressive definition that foregrounds social infrastructure, supports low-carbon investment, and advances decolonisation through greater equity and opportunity.

As a necessary step to address the intellectual and social legacies of colonialism within economics, the economics curriculum needs to be decolonised. Economics remains resistant to change, despite its centrality of Eurocentrism and racial inequality. Arntsen, Puntha, and Gayana Welaratne call for an education that equips students with a decolonial lens, involving them in reimagining the curriculum while integrating decarbonisation and sustainability. Given the links between economic activity, inequality, and environmental harm, a decolonised decarbonisation curriculum is vital for climate justice and for enabling socially engaged, critical graduates. The chapter encourages reflective practitioners, reimagining the economics curriculum, to cultivate graduates equipped to contribute to a more just and sustainable world.

Taken together, these contributions highlight how dominant decarbonisation approaches risk reinforcing colonial injustices if underlying economic structures remain unchallenged. The argument is not that decarbonisation should be avoided or that net-zero strategies are unthinkable, but that visions of the future must extend beyond dystopian predictions flooding media. These visions need to engage with questions of justice that transcend geographic country boundaries. Without an understanding of the economic structures of coloniality, strategies, and policies risk reproducing the historical-structural processes that fuel socio-environmental conflicts and land disputes. A consistent request throughout the book is the need to interrogate the dominant worldview, what is considered knowledge, and the effects that these have on environmental processes. A broader conceptualisation of knowledge, a more diverse set of worldviews, and a more pluralistic set of approaches is crucial not only for economics but for achieving a just decarbonisation. The book has argued that there is a need for stronger incorporation of reparations as part of policy formation and that economic development needs to be redefined to respect ecological boundaries, prioritise redistribution, and incorporate diverse worldviews.

This book is not meant to be prescriptive but rather serves as a resource for developing practice. Addressing the climate crisis offers a crucial chance to rethink and reshape our economic and social systems. It has sparked increasing engagement with movements converging to envision decolonial and ecological development. A common thread running through the chapters is the call for change that avoids locking in systems which reinforce inequality and create further environmental damage. What emerges is an appeal for ambitious decolonisation of the decarbonisation process, treating climate justice as vital in the transition. This will necessarily be a continuing process where each step towards improvement brings new obstacles but also countless opportunities.

References

Bhambra, G. K. (2023). *Rethinking modernity: Postcolonialism and the sociological imagination* (2nd ed.). Palgrave Macmillan.

IPCC. (2023). *Climate change 2023: Synthesis report. Contribution of working groups I, II and III to the sixth assessment report of the intergovernmental panel on climate change* [Core Writing Team, H. Lee and J. Romero (Eds.)]. Geneva, Switzerland.

Sultana, F. (2022). Critical climate justice. *The Geographical Journal, 188*(1), 118–124.

Zografos, C. (2022). The contradictions of green new deals: Green sacrifice and colonialism. *Soundings, 80*(80), 37–50.

Index

A. Agunsoye and A. Arntsen (eds.), *Decarbonising and Decolonising Economics*, https://doi.org/10.1007/978-3-032-11972-8

GPSR Compliance

The European Union's (EU) General Product Safety Regulation (GPSR) is a set of rules that requires consumer products to be safe and our obligations to ensure this.

If you have any concerns about our products, you can contact us on ProductSafety@springernature.com

In case Publisher is established outside the EU, the EU authorized representative is:

Springer Nature Customer Service Center GmbH
Europaplatz 3
69115 Heidelberg, Germany

Batch number: 10245373

Printed by Printforce, the Netherlands